Decatur-Lakeview High School:

A Practical Application of the Trump Plan

Every man who knows how to read has it in his power to magnify himself, to multiply the ways in which he exists, to make his life full, significant and interesting.
Aldous Huxley

Decatur-Lakeview High School:

Englewood Cliffs, N. J.

David W. Beggs, III

Indiana University
Bloomington, Indiana

Former Principal
Lakeview High School
Decatur, Illinois

A Practical Application
of the Trump Plan

Prentice-Hall, Inc.

DECATUR-LAKEVIEW HIGH SCHOOL:
A PRACTICAL APPLICATION OF THE TRUMP PLAN

© 1964 BY

PRENTICE-HALL, INC.

ENGLEWOOD CLIFFS, N. J.

PRINTED IN THE UNITED STATES OF AMERICA
19707—B&P

This book is affectionately dedicated

       to . . . . JoAnn, a supporting partner, who understood

       to . . . . the Lakeview staff, who made it all possible

       to . . . . high school students everywhere, for whom it was done

The rung of a ladder was never meant to rest upon, but only to hold a man's foot long enough to enable him to put the other somewhat higher.

Thomas H. Huxley

Foreword

PROVOCATIVE books are an obvious benchmark of our times. Climbing the highest mountain, rocketing into space, becoming familiar with new countries on this planet, solving tough problems in human relations, learning better how to live with ourselves—these and many other subjects are producing exciting reading for people who, stimulated by television and mass media reviews, are reading more than ever before.

This story of the Decatur-Lakeview Plan fits the mood and tempo of these times.

For the educational professional—this book is as exciting as the latest report of space travel because it too charts the way to new dimensions in what has been chosen as a life work. Whether you are an elementary, secondary, or university teacher, administrator, or researcher, there are realistic ideas challenging you in this volume.

For the layman interested in education—these are ideas to challenge your thinking as you participate in the development of educational policies for the schools in your community. There are ideas that could lift PTA programs to a higher level, board of education meetings to more productive planes, give the Education Committee of the Chamber of Commerce a worthwhile project, and provide a variety of women's clubs and service organizations something constructive to do.

For the courageous educator—reading what other courageous persons have done in one school setting can give support to you and to others and also provide a checklist for comparing what you are doing.

For the cautious—you may find courage to embark on experimentation and innovation because a road map is provided that identifies some possible wrong turns, suggests the right way, and provides encouragement through the testimony of some imaginative people who have made the trip.

For the skeptic—the volume testifies brilliantly that it can be done.

For the educational critic—the book constructively suggests that there are better ways of improving education than what some of you are now suggesting: improvement by subtracting some services or students; improvement by adding more money, more buildings, more teachers, and continuing to do more of the same things as present; and improvement by making some minor readjustments. You will find here frank recognition that *basic changes* are needed and can be done to improve the quality of education without calling for more teachers, more tax money, more homework and the immediate reorganization in teacher education.

The key sentence in the volume occurs when David Beggs says, "If you question this, try it and see!"

David Beggs and his colleagues at Decatur-Lakeview—the students, the teachers, the citizens—have a story to tell and you will enjoy following the narrative. What is more important, you will never be quite the same person when you finish reading the book.

Washington, D.C.   J. LLOYD TRUMP
Associate Secretary
National Association of Secondary-School Principals

Preface

LATELY much has been said and written in professional meetings and journals about the need for looking at ways to get at increased quality in our secondary schools. Often these declarations are based on abstract discussions. This report is quite the opposite. Here is an account of what actually occurred in a typical school in a Midwestern industrial city when the staff changed its instructional methods.

Believing that educational opportunities for high school students could be improved, the staff at Lakeview High School, Decatur, Illinois, inaugurated a new organizational pattern for instruction based on large group and small group instruction and independent study. This is known as the Decatur-Lakeview Plan.

The purpose in recounting these experiences is to offer

a background for consideration for others interested in re-examining both the form and the substance of the secondary schools. The successes and failures of the program at Lakeview may be a backdrop for further innovations in the public schools in flexible scheduling and team teaching.

This is not a "cook book" and care is being taken to caution others not to use this as a definitive guide for adoption elsewhere. Instead, the Decatur-Lakeview Plan is a model from which elements can be taken in structuring other flexible, team-teaching programs. To dogmatize in any such experimental program is to pervert the real purpose of an experimental demonstration. Every community, each school—like every individual—has needs different in degree from all other schools. The task of the leadership in all schools is to develop a program best suited to the youngsters it serves and the staff it employs. If others can profit from the tentative conclusions and experiences at Lakeview, then this book will have met its purpose.

No dramatic claims are made for the success of the Decatur-Lakeview Plan other than that it has increased opportunities for students and stimulated interest in the teaching task among the staff. Lakeview students have not been transformed into intellectual giants, but they have accepted an increased responsibility for learning. Teachers with professional weakness have not been born anew, but they have been able to concentrate on their individual areas of teaching strength.

Basically, the Decatur-Lakeview Plan is a system of instruction employing:

- team teaching
- large and small group instruction with independent study
- multimedia teaching aids
- flexible scheduling

There are seldom simple solutions for complex problems. Such is true with the broad concern of providing for universality and excellence in the public schools. To change the structure for learning in a school or to alter the methods of instruction is of little significance if the essence of learning itself, the involvement of the learner, is not positively influenced. This is a discussion of how one school sought a better way for students to learn and teachers to teach.

Like all pilot programs, the Decatur-Lakeview Plan cannot fail, regardless of whether the test of time proves or disproves the feasibility of the Plan. Honest experimentation does not imply that a predetermined answer must be reached, for a pilot program is one in which a hypothesis is tested. If the hypothesis is proven incorrect or if the Plan is non-operative, the study is still a success.

The Decatur-Lakeview Plan, founded on the recommendations of Dr. J. Lloyd Trump, is an answer to the critics of public education who decry the defensive position taken by modern educators who, according to such critics, bury their heads in the sands of the past. This demonstration project is just one example of the educator's quest for quality educational opportunities for a diverse student population. The Decatur-Lakeview Plan is an action program.

This account is presented as a challenge to others to take bolder steps in individualizing instruction to attain even better quality in our schools.

Acknowledgment

S PECIAL credit is mandatory for J. Lloyd Trump for the thoughtful work he has done in encouraging a re-examination of how we teach in our schools. Although the Decatur-Lakeview Plan does not encompass all of Dr. Trump's recommendations as set forth in his *Images of the Future,*[1] it does embody the basal elements of the Trump recommendations. American public education owes a debt of gratitude to Dr. Trump for his constructive approach in presenting recommendations to bring about increased quality educational opportunities for a diverse school population. He should, of course, be absolved from all the flaws in the fabric of this demonstration school's operation. He created the mold but he did not select the metal.

[1] Trump, J. Lloyd, *Images of the Future,* Commission on the Experimental Study of the Utilization of the Staff in the Secondary School, Urbana, Illinois, 1959.

Mention should also be made of the National Association of Secondary-School Principals' Association's Commission for the Study of the Utilization of Staff in the Secondary School. Two modest grants totaling five thousand eight hundred dollars made possible the faculty summer workshops which were instrumental in developing the program in detail and in setting the stage for its ultimate inauguration.

In any school district the tone is set and the atmosphere for expanding additional effort is created by the board of education. Decatur is richly endowed with a policy-making authority which gave attention to better and new approaches to learning. The Decatur Board of Education granted a five-year period of operation for the Decatur-Lakeview Plan in the summer of 1960.

The teaching task demands time, effort and energy in any normal situation. There is, of course, an added burden in any reorganization work assumed by the teaching staff. The lion's share of credit for the Decatur-Lakeview Plan goes to the Lakeview teachers who went the extra mile in thinking, in formulating, in planning and in working.

Credit needs to be assigned to the building administrators who struggled with mechanics and never were without time to help staff. James L. Olivero, now at Stanford University, was the assistant principal who kept the machinery oiled until he departed in July, 1962. Mr. Olivero made the difference between success and failure during the Plan's early stages. William Fromm assumed Mr. Olivero's position and effectiveness as assistant principal until he took over the principal's duties in January, 1963. Two stalwarts of the service agency of administration who have been a part of the planning and operation were Mrs. Velda Redlich and Mr. Melvin J. Hoffman. Together these skilled professionals demonstrated that team effort has a productive application in secondary school administration.

Gratitude must be expressed to all who had direct or indirect influences on this report. Lee D. Pigott, Decatur's Principal Emeritus, gave encouragement when it was needed. Donald Manlove, secondary school expert and professor at Indiana University, sharpened this report's focus. Peter Casagranda, Indiana University, gave helpful editorial criticism.

William Rogge, University of Illinois staff member, was a provocative consultant during the summer workshop and throughout the school year.

Any fault which exists is the author's, yet any value of the book is to be shared with all those who had direct and indirect influences.

DAVID W. BEGGS, III
Indiana University
Bloomington, Indiana

Contents

Part
One

Ideas
Out of Seclusion

*Every idea is an incitement. It offers itself for be-
lief and if believed it is acted on unless some other
belief outweighs it or some failure of energy
stifles the movement at its birth.*
Justice O. W. Holmes

Chapter One

The Background of the Decatur-Lakeview Plan

W HAT small potatoes we all are, compared with what we might be," Charles Dudley Warner once wrote. The abiding task of the school is to help each of us be the most of what we can be.

While it is easy to pontificate on what is wrong with American public education, it is another matter to set into motion action proposals to do something about our concerns. The staff of Lakeview High School was not content to live with its feelings of anxiety about its instructional program. True, the school enjoyed a good reputation. The belief definitely prevailed that the Lakeview program was nearly as good as it could be within its traditional organizational framework. The drop-out rate decreased sixteen per cent in four years; the number of students going to college tripled in the same period. Interest in scholastic matters steadily increased. Yet this wasn't enough. To do the job the staff felt needed to be done students had to be freed from the lock-step rigidity of the self-contained classroom.

The overriding desire on the part of the staff was to find a better way to individualize instruction. Quality educational opportunities were sought for every Lakeview youngster. The idea of group instruction had to be broken down. Individual education had to begin. Students may be taught in groups, but they learn singly. A way had to be devised, the staff felt, to free the individual learner from the harness that group learning often creates. The practical limits of human and financial resources had to be honored. The Decatur School District was not an affluent one.

With their heads in the clouds and feet on the ground, the Lakeview faculty members sought ways to make the ideal practicable.

Usually when schools want to change their operating procedures for the benefit of youngsters, they institute new requirements or divest themselves of old ones. The pendulum of educational practice swings back and forth. Sometimes there exist more student requirements, sometimes less. The attitude adopted at Lakeview was that if a school was going to be significantly better, it would have to be substantially different. That is, if students were to be given instructional advantages superior to the high level they were already getting, some major alterations would be necessary in the organization for learning.

No apology was made for the splendid work the staff had done over the years. As a matter of fact, only people secure in feeling their professional house was in good order could afford to seek bold advances into new horizons.

The Setting

Lakeview is just one school in the large Decatur School District. It is the smallest of the secondary schools, with one thousand and forty pupils in grades seven through twelve. The central office of the Decatur Schools is a complete one, but not actively involved in the program of instruction on the building level. The school dis-strict supports a quality professional staff. It is the third largest system in Illinois, with over twenty-two thousand students.

The salary compensation for all personnel is competitive in the area. Somehow the Lakeview staff attracted above-average teachers with a commitment to widespread improvement in the school. Hiring is done in the Decatur Schools by the individual principals in cooperation with the assistant superintendent. The principal then is responsible for the quality of staff members in the building.

The superintendent of schools gave latitude to the Decatur-Lakeview Plan by not holding the school to the rigid form of the other schools. The central office staff received all faculty bulletins, had frequent reports of what was going on, but they stayed pointedly out of the way as the Plan was developed and implemented. Sole responsibility was placed on the Lakeview staff for the Plan's evolvement and implementation. The central office officers seldom visited the school, but they did give the Plan psychic encouragement.

This experience gives strength to the proposition that schools will or will not, according to their own volition, develop and change their program and procedures. The basis of school improvement begins and must be carried on at the building level. This is not to minimize the role the central office staff can play in any large or even small school system. It is, however, to put responsibility squarely on the building administrators for encouraging or discouraging improvement practices. Perhaps even more than money, the public secondary schools need creative innovators who will actively seek better ways for youngsters to learn and teachers to teach.

The Past Is Too Much With Us

A review of the history of American public education reveals that we teach pretty much today as was taught one, two, even four generations ago. One teacher meets with twenty to thirty pupils for equal amounts of time each day in all subject areas. This falsely suggests that it takes as long to learn how to drive a nail as it does to understand the syntax of a foreign language. For too long the schools have been treating unequal subject areas as equals.

The teacher has long been a "Jack of all trades." He presents ideas, but too often only facts. He works with students, in one undefined way or another. He evaluates individual accomplishment, sometimes by a standard which is only mythical. In doing countless routine clerical chores not related vitally to helping students learn, the teacher has filled his day.

For too long teachers have operated in a deadening intellectual isolation. During or after their work with students, they have little contact on the professional level with other teachers, other adults who can help in the teaching process. The most contact teachers get with one another is in the teachers' lounges. Sharing ideas on common instructional matters is coincidental in the traditional teacher's ordinary day. Faculty meetings often degenerate to announcement sessions. The wide vistas of educational psychology go unexamined in many faculties' formal meetings. Teachers' institutes, usually held twice a year for all teachers, are a hang-over from a day gone by when there was a need to bring together all the one-room school masters. The talk then was about the school calendar, salaries, textbooks and other matters extraneous to the teaching-learning process. The institutes originally were intended to do for teachers what college preparation does today. Still the institutes go on. Once they were established by law, only a catastrophe of civilization could abandon them.

Concerns About Teaching and Learning

Lakeview teachers wanted to know more about new theories of learning. The teachers were concerned about understanding and fascinated by the potential of technological teaching aids and programmed instruction. While they used films and some other aids to instruction, some question arose as to the real effectiveness of the newer media in instruction. No one can discover the applications of the newer media any better than teachers on the firing line of day-to-day instruction. A self-imposed desire to do this was taken on by a few Lakeview teachers.

Of paramount concern was an increased understanding of the theories of learning and their practical application. Regardless of the motive of the teacher, learning doesn't take place unless the procedures used in teaching are appropriate for student understanding.

A few staff members had been concentrating on the study of the classical concepts of learning. After some general but lively discussion, it was agreed that a system of instruction was needed which would be based on a systematic theory of learning. The point was: We needed to perform the teaching task in a way that maximum learning would take place for each student, regardless of native ability.

One seasoned teacher of English said, "I taught the rules of composition in the best way I could to all my classes, yet one class just didn't understand." Why?

Another teacher with less experience and academic preparation for teaching composition had a class doing superior work in expository writing. Why?

Somehow it didn't seem possible. The expert teacher wasn't as successful as the less experienced teacher.

Several visits to both classes revealed that the more experienced teacher was lecturing in a clear, logical manner. The younger teacher, however, didn't spend much time in class explanations; she discussed students' work with small groups or with individual students. The implications needed validation. Do students learn more by the trial and error method with supporting help than by listening to formal lectures? What place does crisp logical content presentation have in instruction?

About the same time the science department carried off a disproportionate number of honor winners in a science fair. The charge was made by a principal in another participating school that the Lakeview teachers were spending all their time in preparing students for this event. A look at the standardized test scores in science revealed that this couldn't be altogether true. The Lakeview science students were doing very well in achievement as contrasted to the norms in their measured ability. That is, Lakeview students of all abilities were scoring well above the average on the nationwide tests.

Discussions with the science teachers substantiated the fact that all science instruction wasn't consumed with contest preparation. The students did spend class time on their projects, but this was only a fraction of the time they were devoting to individual science study. We asked why these students did so well in both the number and quality of science fair entries. The answer came loud and clear over and over: They understood the scientific subject matter and liked to use it. Once again we wondered why the students liked science as well as they did. Did not the students in the other schools find the same content equally as intriguing? Why didn't the same Lakeview students enjoy social studies as much as they did science? Why did some teachers' students do significantly more work in science projects than others?

Questions, questions, questions!

A visit to a world history class one day revealed that a splendid lecture was given on the philosophies of the medieval period. The atmospere was electric. The students were enraptured. The next class we visited was another world history teacher's group. The content was nearly the same but the presentation was dull. The students were apathetic, barely polite in giving attention. Somehow it didn't seem that this was the same subject, much less the same course. Why not?

The Germ of the Pilot Study

About this time the assistant-to-the-principal, a delightful lady of vision, came into the meeting of the school's administrators with a booklet written by a man named J. Lloyd Trump. This was a paper-bound booklet entitled *Images of the Future*. She read from it and attached a routing sheet to it so all could read what Dr. Trump had to say. Dr. Trump made a series of recommendations about the way a school should be organized. There was little reaction to her report. How, the department heads wondered, could a school use the ideas put forth in this outlandish violation of all that they knew and had been doing?

At the next meeting only one other person read the booklet. The assistant-to-the-principal asked that it be passed along. It was. By the next administrative meeting all nine department heads had read it. Some of the ideas had an appeal.

A lengthy discussion followed and logic fell into place. Perhaps there was wisdom in considering a reorganization of instructional procedures. Manufacturing procedures had changed since the Industrial Revolution, maybe we needed an Instructional Revolution!

How could we expect real quality in education if every teacher was expected to be equally expert at all phases of the teaching process? Of course there was advantage in having teachers work together on common problems in a team situation, but how could we do it at Lakeview?

Why shouldn't one staff member concentrate in depth with his content area and, therefore, strengthen his teaching? Our thoughts went back to our earlier observations. Naturally it followed that the English students who were doing so well had the opportunity to try, to fail, and to try again. They were learning by actually writing, not by listening to lectures about writing.

The reason the science students did well became apparent. They were doing work which interested them and were, therefore, willing to give the extra effort to work on science projects.

Then, too, we understood why the first world history class visited was so much superior to the second. The first teacher had a great fluency with colorful words. He had an unusual facility for transmitting thoughts. Obviously these two history teachers were in possession of a different degree of skill in idea presentation. Both had similar content preparation. Both were rated as good teachers.

Agreements Were Reached

Subsequent administrative meetings concentrated on the strengths and weaknesses of the instructional opportunities youngsters had at Lakeview. Furthermore, the department heads involved their teachers in similar discussions of teaching and learning.

Cement was put around the belief that we wanted to work to continue to reduce the drop-out rate and keep all students, irrespective of ability, in school. We wanted the principle of universal educational opportunity to be a reality. Equally important, the staff felt, was the continuation of high-level academic experiences for our able and ambitious learners. We wanted a way to get our lip-service into action.

Next we took a look at ourselves, the professional staff. We agreed that some teachers were better at lecturing while others worked better with individual students or small groups. A visit to almost any class pointed up the fact that a group of thirty was too large for a really successful discussion. We needed smaller classes to get all students involved in the class discussions. Students seldom questioned other students and little brain-storming went on in our traditional classes. They were often teacher dominated. Questions asked, answers given. The sequence was repeated over and over. Was this the best way to learn?

Learning doesn't take place by talking or by listening alone. Action is needed. Students need to read, to construct or reconstruct, to marshal facts. They must develop concepts or broad understandings to master knowledge and to develop skills. Mathematics is not learned by listening or talking about the theorems; problems have to be confronted. Typing isn't learned by listening to a discussion about the keyboard, but by practicing on a machine. Learning, then, is a combination of listening, discussing and above all—doing.

The Big Question: How?

How could we arrange the school program so all these activities would go on in each subject area? We would have to do violence to tradition in order to get at a new, better system of instruction. We would have to supply students with the opportunity to hear quality lectures, to meet for discussion, and to work independently. Sometimes the sequence necessarily would be different. Sometimes students would need to work on their own before the small discussion group met. Although the sequence of activity would vary from time to time and from content to content, the vital elements of good instruction would be constant. Student involvement in the learning process was the key.

We decided upon the idea to employ our staff so as to let the teacher do that at which he was best. It sounded so easy to agree upon, but how would it work at Lakeview? If one teacher of business education, for example, was best at giving lectures on bookkeeping procedures, then this teacher would give all the lectures on bookkeeping. Since listening is a highly personalized and individual activity we reasoned it would make little difference if one or two hundred or more students were present; sometimes students would need to meet in large groups.

If a teacher had a particular skill in stimulating discussion, was good at listening, and knew where to get in and out of the group discussion, then it seemed logical to have this teacher concentrate on working with small groups of students. Students would, at other times, need to meet in intimate discussion groups with a skilled teacher.

Immediately it was clear that members of the staff would have to pool their talents and work in concert if the full potential of individuals within the group was to be molded into a coordinated system of instruction. Teaching teams were needed. One teacher would handle certain functions of the instructional process and another would handle others. Both would work together to lock their activities into a related pattern. Thus, teaching teams were established.

The isolation of the classroom was broken by this combination of talents. More than one teacher would be working with each group of students. Defoe pointedly depicted social progress when he brought the Man Friday to Robinson Crusoe's island of isolation. The same social elevation took place in teaching when teachers joined in teaching teams. New and richer relationships were needed. Cooperative effort was demanded.

The Other Elements

The professional literature was replete with ideas on how students could benefit from listening to tapes of significant presentations, using learning programs with profit and increasing understanding by seeing ideas presented visually. How did all of this fit into the other proposals for better instruction that were flying about? Students needed time to do these things during the school day, and the addition of more things for a student to do didn't seem realistic. Lakeview students were already busy.

Another shift in tradition based on sound reason was necessary. The comments of an industrial arts teacher freed the staff thought pattern. He said that it didn't take as long to learn woodworking as it did electricity. Yet he said he would like to have the woodworking students in class for two hours and the electricity students only forty minutes or less. In addition, he wanted to meet with the electricity students in the shop for a one-and-a-half-hour block of time. His point was well taken. The lengths and frequency of classes should vary, for assignment of time should be based on the needs of learning activity.

The concept was projected and we found that teachers had different time requirements for various courses. Some classes needed to meet daily, others didn't. No harness should be put on one that didn't fit another. Lecture periods needed to meet for less time than discussion sessions. In some courses one or two lectures each week were appropriate, whereas in other content areas more lectures were necessary.

When the teachers of different subjects met they agreed that it didn't take as much time for students to master one subject as another. They said, too, that some courses required more lectures than discussion sessions and the converse for others. Independent study time was also felt to be needed in varying durations for different subjects. The limits could seldom be set, but the staff believed that the school day should be divided between independent study, large group and small group time.

Students have so little time in school and must cover so much that it is unjust to assume that all subjects require equal time. The time schedule of classes must vary.

This man Trump made sense to the Lakeview staff.

A Label Put on the Systems

After all these and other considerations had been made, a program of instruction was put together. For want of a better name it was called the Decatur-Lakeview Plan.

Basically the Decatur-Lakeview Plan involved:

1. Large group instruction for content presentation.

2. Independent study for individual work.

3. Small group activity for discussion and idea reinforcement.

4. Team teaching to bring the combined talents of teachers together in common instructional problems.

5. Use of technological aids and programmed instruction wherever possible to stimulate and clarify learning.

6. Varied time allotments for different courses and diverse learning groups.

The Problem of the Mechanics

We consulted school people from near and far and we distributed the prospectus of the program rather widely. Moreover, we studied the critical evaluations very carefully.

Some educators said these elements couldn't be combined into a program, for they maintained that a student body couldn't be scheduled in such a manner. They said it was philosophically sound but practically impossible. But experience has shown this isn't so. Though one approach is described in the Decatur-Lakeview Plan for scheduling students and teachers, the innovators see several other possibilities. Too often all of the educators of America have allowed administrative convenience to be an obstacle to educational advancement. The work of schedule construction is, admittedly, a difficult one. It is, however, one of the most important functions a principal fulfills, for he brings students and teachers together through scheduling, he sets the limits and opens the many opportunities for effective learning. In spite of its difficulty, more consideration needs to be given to scheduling procedures employed in the schools.

Data processors, systems consultants, and creative administrators are all means to solving the problem of the mechanics of doing what we know is best, bringing students and teachers together for learning and teaching. The consideration has too long been obscured. It is not what can we do, but what will we do to make learning more effective. The school schedule must be determined by the needs of students, not by senseless standards of rigidity.

Inequality of Equality

The Decatur-Lakeview Plan is a wholesale attack on the concept that it is proper to treat unequal subjects as equals. For too long educational procedure has regarded all subjects as equal, with a common distribution of time; all students as equal, with the same demands for content mastery and development; and all teachers as equal, with equal numbers of hours, of students, and of preparation time—regardless of professional need!

Countless discussions are required when one adjusts any segment of the school program. The final responsibility rests with the building principal, but he must get the best thinking and inspire the support of the professional staff.

The Decatur-Lakeview Plan puts focus on each course, each teacher, and each student, bonding them together in new and unique ways.

The Staff Did It

Members of the Lakeview staff were solid in their support of the ideals implied by the Decatur-Lakeview Plan. They taught for the benefit of their students; but, at the same time, they saw the implications for other students and teachers in different schools.

A school of one thousand forty pupils is more than thirty-four one-room schools with sixty-nine teachers. The Lakeview staff responded to the call for excellence. They broke down these single room boundaries and agreed they wanted to be on the cutting edge of progress in education. To do this the staff attended workshops for curriculum consideration in the summer, went to evening classes in the winter, and took part in the deliberations of professional organizations.

Lakeview teachers showed their personal desire to be better teachers by their work. They went from the verbal level to the action level in curriculum investigation. This accounts for the nineteen articles in print in professional journals, the four leadership positions, the thirty-seven speaking roles on educational meeting panels, and the seventeen other organizational responsibilities that Lakeview staff members filled during the inauguration of the Decatur-Lakeview Plan.

One cannot talk about Lakeview without speaking about its students. The entire motive for the Plan was to give all the students as much as any school could offer in terms of quality educational offerings. The students responded. Without a doubt, the total group was receptive and involved in these new educational opportunities. The center of life, not only from eight to four, but during evening and weekend hours, was the school and its programs.

The Decatur-Lakeview Plan is one answer to the problem of achieving excellence in the schools and, at the same time, providing significant instruction for all the children of all the people.

Chapter
Two

How We Believe
People Learn

IF there is anything public school people talk too little about, it is the process by which adolescents learn. The concepts of varying class size and flexible scheduling in the Decatur-Lakeview Plan find their rationale in a set of beliefs about how learning, knowing, understanding and recalling take place.

It is not enough to teach as we were taught. Schools of the past were organized around an attitude about learning supported mostly by conjecture and a tradition of convenience. The significance of the Boston Latin Grammar School's contribution to education in 1643 was not, as time would seem to show, its lock-step pattern of chronological grades of organization; but the Boston Latin Grammar School should be remembered because it was the first in the

United States to systematize instruction and because it brought learners to a place called school. The Boston Latin School, to be sure, was a bold first step, but it was only a step. Too much time has elapsed since other advances in organization for learning have taken place. The Boston Latin School was a stimulus for an era, not a model for all time.

Froebel, in the eighteenth century, knew a great deal about flexible scheduling, the topic many today regard as novel. Schools of the period influenced by Froebel were more similar to the organization of the Decatur-Lakeview Plan than to the traditional organizational form found in the United States since the founding of the Boston Latin Grammar School.

The field of educational psychology is in its dark ages, even though in recent years great strides have been made in learning more about learning. Where was physical science in its development thirty, twenty or even ten years ago? The accumulation of new and vital scientific information of this decade has been without precedent in both depth and abundance. Educators must keep abreast of the progress made in the science of learning and make decisions accordingly; lively interest in educational research is a healthy characteristic.

Getting From Theory to Practice

The aim of the curriculum worker as he operates in the public school is to make it possible for principles of effective learning to be put into regular operation in the classroom. The curriculum worker needs to determine what are the actual outcomes of any form of instruction given. Hundreds of books have given the descriptions of how learning should take place in the schools; countless research studies have isolated significant variables in the educative process; and several major flaws in the public school's lack of ability to provide fully for individual differences have been recounted thousands of times. Yet we go on in much the same way as we have since 1643. True, we have refined the imperfect fabric of graded instruction for all students by means of various ability-grouping systems. Other improvements in staff training and facilities have made the public school of our time better than those of a generation ago. But this is not good enough.

A searching and continuing reappraisal of our patterns of school organization must be made, and this reappraisal must be based on the best we can find from the expanding body of knowledge about learning.

Any discussion of learning theories in a presentation such as this will suffer from brevity. Some attention must be given, however, to the theory of learning behind the Decatur-Lakeview Plan or its basal element is lost.

Learning as a Result of Hard Work

At one time it was assumed the mind was like a muscle, and that hard work alone would develop mental powers. This theory contended that the harder and more distasteful the work was for the learner, the better. Concern was not given to the practicality of a subject in determining what subjects students should study. The only yardstick was its academic rigor. From this school of thought came the notion that the study in equal lengths of time of ancient history, languages, mathematics and science was the business of all students.

An outgrowth of this theory is the belief that bright youngsters should be in souped-up classes. Often these classes do twice as many problems in mathematics, for example, as youngsters of average ability. The recommendations that bright students do more work is a basic premise of those who believe in the "muscle" theory of learning.

People of this school usually think that learners are different only in their interest, motivation or home-background and ignore the differences in basic mental facility. The difference humans have in conceptual ability and in interests escaped those who subscribed to this theory.

Learning as a Result of Maximum Exposure

The pendulum of time swung and another misconception dominated the schools. This was the theory of learning which held that the mind was like a pitcher, and that education was the process of filling the pitcher. Thus, teachers talked and talked and talked to fill the pitcher. Little concern was given to what was taught, in the belief that no facts were unimportant and that once one had enough information, intelligence would necessarily be the result. The teacher who insists that the textbook is the bible and that it must, therefore, be covered in detail believes in this theory.

Schools which stressed memorization of poetry, formulas, titles, rules, and laws flourished, thus adding strength to the belief this was learning. The flaw is that the power of memorization is not necessarily the hallmark of an educated man.

Learning as the Result of Transfer of Generalizations

Another belief about learning was proposed by the school which held that an idea or concept can, once it is learned, be transferred to a different but similar situation. The transfer theory of learning gave credit to teaching moral lessons in literature, for instance, so as to provide a background for operation in later life. A survey of any penal institution's inmates and their early childhood reading habits would tend to discredit this theory.

Algebra was taught because it was felt that the understanding of unknowns in a mathematical formula would help learners face unknowns in the uncertainties of later life. Adherents to this point of view were principle-oriented. That is, they had an interest in teaching the laws and theories accepted by them as eternal truths. The scientific method, inductive and deductive thinking, and "morality" of the Judeo-Christian tradition were the foundations of instruction.

The flaw here is that ideas and arrangements of facts or knowledge in the physical, mathematical or social sciences are not always applicable to a different situation. Students *may* transfer the deductive reasoning process learned in mathematics to an economic problem, but there is no guarantee of this. While some instances in which transfer of knowledge and ideas does take place and can be cited, there is no universal tendency to support a system of instruction based on the transfer theory.

Learning as the Response of a Structured Stimulus

About the time that the transfer theory of learning was being doubted by even its strongest supporters, the most highly developed process of learning, at this point in time, was the product of Edward Thorndike and his followers. Thorndike felt people learned (reacted) as a result of a stimulus. He maintained that for each given stimulus there was a subsequent response. The teacher's job was, therefore, to provide a stimulus which would evoke a desired response. It was assumed that if the correct stimulus were chosen, a predeterminable and unvarying response would result.

The value of Thorndike's work has been translated into worthwhile application by the designers of programmed learning materials. Thorndike further taught that people learn when the acquisition of ideas is based on knowledge previously gained. He wisely counseled teachers to present ideas in such a way that a student would have a feeling of satisfaction in his success at understanding. The valve of motivation in instruction was understood by this school of educational psychology.

The weakness of the stimulus-response theory was its overemphasis on the mechanical aspects of learning. This encouraged too little consideration of individual differences among learners. Repetitive drill in teacher-dominated classes characterized the methods of this school. Many of the obstacles to development of human talent and creativity have come about as the result of rigid reliance on standardized tests as the measure of achievement. In addition, any given stimulus brought about varied responses in learners because of their individual differences.

However, it should be remembered that the stimulus-response school did promote the importance of the learning atmosphere. Advocates viewed behavior change as the goal of learning and became interested in the physical and psychological atmosphere in which instruction takes place.

Learning as an Appeal to the Total Human Organism

The Gestalt psychologists came on the scene with the belief that man is a whole organism and can only be considered through viewing the sum of all his parts. The Gestalt school rejected the mechanical aspect of learning and held that the environment of the learner and association of one human with another resulted in learning. Insight into and understanding of the human mind was the aim of these "organic" psychologists. The central, contribution of this school was its emphasis on the differences in and among individuals. The human organism was thought to be in a state of continual change. At this stage of educational psychology the learner, as an individual, became the center of interest in instruction. Pupil-teacher planning became the order of the day and teachers who subscribed to this notion on learning allowed class time to be dominated by pupil interaction with other pupils.

Learning Theory in the Decatur-Lakeview Plan

The comforting thing about developing an instructional program today is that there is a basis in the various theories of learning on which to build. The educationists of a generation from now will have, without any question, even more to build on as the field of educational psychology continues to develop. Unfortunately, at this point there have been too few massive demonstration projects involving a whole school. While there is value in the tight research studies in which a single variable is considered, the applications of such research are necessarily limited and slow to be adopted. Too much research has been conducted by the educators with a university orientation who use atypical schools in their studies. There exists a need for more demonstration schools to challenge the traditional organization of schools.

After a number of conferences and faculty meeting discussions during the planning year of the Decatur-Lakeview Plan, the following beliefs about how adolescents learn were agreed on:

Belief One—Students learn when they see purpose to learning.

The role of the teacher is to develop understandings of purpose. Reasons for and love of learning usually do not come without guidance and inspiration. The teacher, then, is a director of learning. This is a highly personalized matter for each student and makes the job a complex one for the teacher.

Learning should be goal-oriented to be purposeful and problem-centered to be effective. Educational programs should be thought of in terms of behavior goals for pupils.

Belief Two—Learning is an active process.

Students may hear ideas, be exposed to facts, or see skills demonstrated; but before there is understanding, acquisition of knowledge, or development of abilities, the students must use the facts, ideas or skills. Rather than drill, youngsters must ponder, rearrange and use information and skills before possession becomes reality. Teachers need to encourage students' activities in depth and breadth to facilitate learning and need to give them the time and the space to pursue this active process.

Belief Three—Change in behavior is the central goal of instruction.

If students do not grow, develop, adapt, create, and change in their behavior as a result of self-realization and understanding, then instruction is ineffectual. Teachers need to ask frequently what behavior change will result as an outgrowth of teacher-dominated instruction. This is where methodology of instruction becomes very important.

Belief Four—Students learn at different rates and on various levels of comprehension in different content areas.

The school's organization for instruction must compensate for the differences among and in pupils. The school should be organized in such a way that the able and ambitious learner is not harnessed by the slow learner. On the other hand, the slow learner is a learner and respect for his rate and depth of understanding must be maintained. All students should be able to move from where they are to the outer limits of where they can go during any given year of instruction.

Belief Five—Students learn best as a result of the appeal to the senses: seeing, hearing, touching and smelling.

Effective instruction employs as many of the senses as possible on each idea presented. The implication in this belief of a high degree of visual communication is clear. A multisensory approach to instruction is necessary.

Belief Six—The environments for learning, psychological and physical, are contributing to successful outcomes.

An atmosphere in which an adolescent is secure, wanted, and appreciated contributes to the energy and enthusiasm he puts into his educational activities. Students should be grouped in such a way that the result is a feeling of acceptance and satisfaction on the part of each of the members. The implication here is that one should really know students before determining their learning group in each subject area. There are many bases for grouping. Sometimes students are grouped by their mental aptitude, sometimes by their achievement, sometimes by verbal ability, sometimes by vocational choice, sometimes by emotional equivalency, and sometimes by other criteria.

Physical facilities are a barrier or aid to learning. Chairs, rooms, heat, lights and equipment should be arranged or used so as to increase learning potential.

Belief Seven—Learning is affected by the student's concept of himself and his attitude toward others.

Students can do little that they think they cannot do. Before one can set a realistic educational goal, he must see himself as worthy and able to achieve success in specific and routine tasks. A student must see himself as one who can do what he aspires to do.

Care must be taken to insulate adolescents against the adverse effects of unflattering comparison with others.

The atmosphere of the learning group is either a contributing or detracting factor to formal learning in school. Caution should be made in imposing rules and imposing requirements while maintaining a balance of fairness, firmness and friendliness in establishing a consistent behavior structure.

The Beliefs in Action

Identifying beliefs about how students learn is one thing, but fitting staff behavior and administrative patterns into the framework of these principles is a task. A visit to a teacher's class who had spoken of the need for action in the learning process revealed that this teacher prevented action on the students' part by lengthy lectures, daily quizzes and classtime reading assignments. Why? Past experience and previous training were so much a part of this teacher's behavior pattern that what she knew and what she did were quite different. The administrative goal, then, was to work with this teacher in bringing her doing up with her knowing. The chapter on in-service education will describe the techniques used for this. The point is this: While we accepted some beliefs about learning, we didn't always employ them in day-to-day instructional practice. This didn't mean the beliefs were wrong, but it meant that as a staff we had to do some changing in our operational behavior in the classroom.

In summary form the relationship between our beliefs and organization for instruction is shown.

Belief	Administrative Organization
ONE—PURPOSEFUL LEARNING	Department heads work with teachers to evaluate the curriculum in terms of its purpose to adolescents. Added preparation time is given to staff members who are going to make presentations by large group programming.
TWO—ACTIVE LEARNING PROCESS	Time in the school day is set aside for independent study. Small groups are set up in which student-centered activity and pupil involvement is emphasized.
THREE—BEHAVIOR CHANGE	Placing more responsibility on students for learning gives increased opportunity to bring about a wholesome behavior change in school. Independent study time does this.

Belief	Administrative Organization
FOUR—VARYING RATE AND DIFFERENT LEVELS	Grouping by ability in small groups, using programmed instruction, tapes and films, and personal assistance in independent study helps make provisions for difference in learners' abilities.
FIVE—MULTISENSORY APPEAL	Large group presentations use overhead transparencies, records, and visual projections. Establishment of a materials center with facilities for viewing and listening helps make this a reality.
SIX—ENVIRONMENT FOR LEARNING	Development of attitude of interest in individuals on the part of the staff and provision, through small group instruction, to get the job done. Remodeled facilities allow space for students to do independent study and for teachers to work together in teams. Use of the school's halls as a museum where art work, sculpture, documents, etc., reflect the school's purpose, add interest and place a new emphasis on the school's heritage.
SEVEN—SELF-CONCEPT AND ATTITUDE TOWARD OTHERS	The self-concept is developed through the interplay of student-to-student activities and by the close associations developed in the small group.

The large groups were expected to be teacher-centered, but students were expected to be actively involved. Here content presentation with a multisensory appeal was the central concern, for the communication was essentially a one-way flow, teacher to learner. The small groups were designed to be student centered, and were to be characterized by a high degree of student involvement through individual participation by discussion and work with teacher or fellow students. Each student was given a large block of time for independent work, during which time he was to prepare for the large and small group activities. It was intended that emphasis be placed on the development of personal responsibility for learning.

Emphasis was placed on students "doing," on executing, on judging, on rearranging, in all of their school activities. Sometimes they read and other times they listened. Always there was a follow-up intended in which they would explain, write or construct. Learning was meant to be an active process for the learner. The teaching job was to get the students involved in mental and mechanical operations.

Chapter
Three

A Planned Program
for Progress

THE best motives in the world won't solve a problem unless they are transformed into a planned program of action.

Historically the concept that the schools belong to the
people and are the peoples' business has meant that educators
—the real experts—have had too little influence on the organization used for instruction. When a patient goes to a doctor,
he listens to the advice he is given. A client of a lawyer takes
the professional counsel he is given. Somehow in the field of
education it is different. Authorities on school operation are
at least a dime a dozen. A certain lack of respect for the
counsel of the educator may be the reason so little pointed
reform has gone on in the schools.

The Problems Ahead

The United States was the first nation to make free education possible for every child through the high school level. In providing opportunities for all, we somehow got the notion that quality instruction would ensue. Quantity and quality aren't necessarily equatable.

As we shift from an agrarian to a technological society the business of education takes on a new dimension. Work for men no longer requires only a strong back and a willing heart. This generation of adolescents is going to live its productive adult years in a world far different from even today's "modern" world. We don't know the issues youngsters will face, but we do know we must teach them to think, to reason, to judge and to create.

As our society changes, so must our schools. We need to do an even finer job of educating tomorrow's citizens today. This doesn't mean that we need more of the same, for we need significantly different learning experiences for our adolescents. The demand is urgent.

The population growth alone is staggering. Between 1900 and 1950 our population doubled, in contrast with the period from 1850 to 1900, when it tripled, and with 1800 to 1850 when it nearly quintupled. The growth rate in America will continue to climb. More and more people will need to be educated.

We must provide for the defense of our land and our beliefs in freedom. To do this we currently spend more each year in national defense than we've spent in any decade on public education. As a nation of wealth, we have accepted our obligations to the less fortunate of the world, and this has been a drain on our purse.

The state, the aggregate of all of us, has exercised the dictates of conscience and accepted the responsibility of providing for those unable to work or to produce and for those past the usual working years. Added to these pressures on national wealth, there are countless governmental agencies to regulate our economy and to assist farmers, transportation networks and scores of other threads of our industrial blanket. On top of this, we have asked for vast internal improvements. All this, needless to say, takes a lot of money.

Education, a public-supported welfare concern, is in competition with all other calls on the American dollar. Educators are, therefore, compelled to look again at how each dollar is spent to see that it is doing the big job the times demand. A searching reappraisal is needed in all aspects of school operation. The Decatur-Lakeview Plan is one school's answer to how school funds may be fully utilized.

The greater reason for taking a critical look at how we teach, however, is related to a continuing quest we must make for quality in our schools. Excellence should be our national goal.

More New Abilities to Be Provided For

The character of the population in our schools is very different from what it was at the century's beginning, even different from that of a decade ago. Today a greater proportion of low ability students stay in school longer, for there is no longer a farm, shop, or a store for the non-academic student to take refuge in. The decline of non-skilled jobs, plus the pressure of society's expectation of education, has kept youngsters in school longer today than previously.

At the same time, we must do a better job of educating the upper ability levels in our society. The future inventors, statesmen, scientists and intellectuals need the full measure of preparation we can give them so their destinies can be fulfilled. More mathematics, perhaps of a different kind, is needed along with a rich exposure to literature, science and social sciences. The arts must not be ignored. Our concern must be for all talent in whatever field or dimension it exists.

Quality in educational opportunity, then, will be achieved when we find a way to help each youngster reach his maximum self-development. The spectrum of individuality is broad, the range is full. Excellence in the schools will only come when we take our sights off groups and center them on individuals.

Success by Individualizing Instruction

The Decatur-Lakeview Plan is a calculated attempt at excellence by giving each youngster a broad and personalized instructional experience.

Students learn by seeing and listening. These processes are done individually. They can learn when listening to one person speak or by tuning in on a nation-wide presidential speech along with thousands of others. We have felt that it makes more sense to bring all students in a single grade level together when it is appropriate to see and hear. As a result of large group lectures, teachers save time. Instead of five lectures a day, they can give one. The rest of the day can be spent in working with students or doing a better job of preparation for the next lecture.

But students don't learn by seeing and listening alone. They learn by doing. They learn as they discuss and as they work through problems. We feel that good discussion can't take place in a group of thirty. Profitable learning discussions require groups of seven to twelve. Therefore, we want youngsters to have maximum opportunities for expressing themselves and for testing their knowledge. A large part of the students' day needs to be in these small groups.

Before one can discuss or profit from listening, he must do independent work. He must read, write, check resources and formulate his own ideas. We have set up a school day which leaves youngsters on their own to study, to reinforce ideas and cultivate skills.

Emphasis on Individualism

A lot has been said about the organization man and the submergence of individuality. There can be no doubt about the trend toward bigness in all phases of human life. But the organization, whether economic, social or political, is no better than the ideas and abilities of its individual members. The demand in big organizations is for people who are big in vision, knowledge and responsibility.

Therefore, the schools must work to teach individuals, not groups. They must seek to develop each adolescent's abilities and skills so that his individual contribution to bigness will be significant.

A primary job of the modern public school is to instill in students a respect for learning and a personal desire for it. We need to free the capacity to learn. The treasures of resources for the next generation are not our oil supplies or our land, but the minds of our young people. The Decatur-Lakeview Plan seeks to develop strong individuals.

Technology and Team Teaching

Technology has become a part of our country's life, yet the schools have done little to adopt it for benefit of learners. Teaching machines, visual projectors, video tapes, and scores of other aides to learning are worth increased consideration on the part of public school educators. Some of these technological supports to education are included in the operation of the Decatur-Lakeview Plan.

For too long we've expected our teachers to be all things to all people. We have sent them to classrooms to work in isolation from other teachers. The Decatur-Lakeview Plan employs team teaching, the practice of bringing the talents of two or more teachers to bear on common instructional problems. For the Plan recognizes that all teachers, regardless of their professional education and personal worth, aren't equally competent at each phase of the teaching process. Therefore, provisions are made for teachers to specialize in those aspects of teaching at which they are the most effective.

Various Elements Make a Coordinated Whole

The Decatur-Lakeview Plan didn't just grow like Topsy. It was carefully structured to meet the needs of a particular staff at a particular time.

Once the problems were isolated, the elements were coordinated. This is not proposed as a model for all schools to emulate. It is, instead, a demonstration that students and teachers can successfully and effectively operate in a different way than they did in the past.

If in another school setting, the innovators might have shaped a different program. The differences would be regulated by resources at hand, by board of education expectations and by community requirements.

This particular project is characterized by a vast amount of staff and community involvement. The community participation never was on the level of professional decisions about how the Plan should be shaped, but it served as a court of criticism. There never was a vote taken by the staff; consensus determined acceptance.

Consultants were used in helping give the faculty and administrators aid in decision-making. Educational psychologists, administrative experts and subject-matter scholars were consulted in person or through their writing as the Plan was pieced together, block by block.

DECATUR-LAKEVIEW PLAN	
Element	*Application*
Large-group, Small-group Instruction	Students sometimes meet in small groups of 7-15 students; sometimes in large groups of up to 200 or more students.
Independent Study	Time in the regular school day provided for independent, self-directed study where students work alone.
Multimedia Teaching Aids	Structured use of visual materials where possible to show as well as tell students of the emphasis on instructional materials center; generous use of audio independent learning.
Team Teaching	Combination of two or more teachers' talents in common instructional problems.
Flexible Scheduling	Learning activities for each course vary and schedule bends to instructional needs.
Facility Reassignment	Individual study carrels; large group instructional areas; small group seminar rooms; learning laboratories.

This account gives scant attention to the academic areas as such. This does not mean little attention was given them in shaping the Decatur-Lakeview Plan, but the assignment here was to present the school's approach to an organization for instruction. Lakeview teachers are scholars of the first rank. The omission of a discussion of the academic discipline is not to diminish their worth in the school's program, but such is not in the province of this report.

The Motive Exposed

Situations don't improve by wishing alone. If the schools are to provide for an expanding and diverse population, plans need to be put forth to get the job done. The talents of our really top-flight teachers should be made available to more students, all agree. Bold projects to bring theory to reality must be considered. Who is in a better position to propose ways to improve education than practicing public school people?

There are quite enough people around to tell educators what they already know about the public schools. The indispensable thing for real progress in education is constructive proposals for fundamental improvement. This the Decatur-Lakeview Plan was intended to be.

The chart gives a bird's eye view of the Plan. Appendix I will show a comparison of class sizes, teacher requirements and time distribution in the Decatur-Lakeview Plan to a traditional schedule.

Decision-Making and Policy Formation

Decision-making is an important part of any faculty's activity. Countless patterns are to be found in practice in secondary schools. However, before there can be real progress in changing a school's program, the way in which decisions are to be made needs to be identified and accepted by all the staff. Lack of clarity on this point is a major stumbling block to the possibility of program improvement.

Progress doesn't happen by chance. It requires professional cooperation and a planned program with accepted channels of communication. Cooperation doesn't become a worthwhile activity until the areas in which and by which it takes place are recognized by a school staff. The building principal is traditionally responsible for defining procedures, for making decisions, and for identifying procedures of formulating policy.

Discussions with a number of administrators concerning decision-making have revealed a general lack of agreement on this important issue. A visit to one of the noted schools of Illinois indicated a clear-cut belief that decision-making was to be vested in "the leader" (in this case, the superintendent in a single high school district). Private discussions with staff members seemed to support this as acceptable and agreeable. This school had both the acknowledged program and the recognized reputation of excellence to support the contention that this was successful. This staff seemed to feel secure with this role of an all-powerful director lodged in the administrator.

At the same time, there was evidence of a permissive atmosphere which encouraged teachers to go to the administrator with ideas, suggestions and concerns. The problem was that the administrator, in this case, was the sole agent for change. The entire school's program was singularly dependent on his ability and interest in all phases of the faculty's operation. This was an acknowledged and apparently a successful pattern, owing to the unusual ability of the chief school officer in this situation with this particular faculty. However, the staff agreed that a change in administrators could drastically impair the school's decision-making process in bringing about improvement and change.

Discussion of this topic with another administrator in an area of high salaries (with supposedly a correspondingly highly competent staff) indicated the decision-making role bounced about with no single recognizable procedure for reaching conclusions or including actions on the school's operation policy. The principal of this building responded by saying: "We haven't got around to identification of decision-making procedures yet. We are too busy keeping school going to consider changing policies or practices." Here again the staff seemed satisfied to go it alone in working within the traditions of the past, although they expressed a desire to be heard on issues of school operation and wished there was some way to influence change in the school's operational policies.

When a staff member was asked why the point wasn't brought up, the logical response came: "How can you bring the topic up if there is the belief that nothing should be changed and that teachers don't develop policies? Anyway," this teacher went on to say, "no one here feels a desire to change anything. It's not that all is perfect, but the attitude toward change or adjustment isn't accepted. We each work in a separate vacuum." This school had little coordination of program or content within a subject area or of methods of instruction.

Obviously, some of the staff felt that the district's salary was more appealing than a sense of professional satisfaction. This was borne out in the lack of knowledge this staff appeared to have about recent content and curriculum advances. The school's alarmingly high drop-out rate, even in a Brahmin community, was of little faculty concern.

The *laissez-faire* atmosphere was typified in a statement made by a physics teacher: "I start all over with basic mathematics. Our mathematics teachers don't know how to teach what *I* want." Somehow the attitude in this school, with its imposing physical structure and favorable teacher-student ratio, was: Each teacher should teach as if a student never had a teacher before and would never have one again. Here was a group of good staff members who were well paid, well trained, and extensively experienced, but there was no evidence of a system of instruction. Little coordination was evident which, if present, could have converted this faculty of soloists into a beautiful instructional symphony. Somehow there was no definition of group goals, no defined relationships between the parts which are the whole of the school.

Boards of education would do well to develop an "effectiveness schedule" to go along with their "salary schedule" in paying teachers. Such an index would measure the actual use of the teaching talents of the districts in regard to specific problems and instructional needs of the students in the school.

The Process of Decision-Making

There was another model, one far more worthwhile for the application at Lakeview. This was the school where teachers were: (1) considered by themselves and by administration to be the source of ideas and policy recommendation; (2) anxious to develop procedures to be understood and accepted by the majority, even when some individual advantage was sacrificed to the common good; (3) receptive to ideas evaluated by their worth, presented by either individual teachers, administrators or resource people in an accepted channel; and (4) concerned about school policy in relation primarily to student welfare. The function of the administration was to identify problems, to involve the staff in decision-making and to inspire the teachers to carry out the recommendations which had been jointly formulated.

Constructive change in a school should be the central concern of a professional staff and the principle concern of the administration— both the observer and catalyst of the over-all program. Not just to change for its own sake, but to improve, to develop, to refine, to adjust, to expand and to explore. Regardless of how well a school is doing in meeting its students' needs, there may be room to do an even better job, to add new or enriched experiences for the student population.

Continuous evaluation is the cornerstone of an on-going school. Frequent looks at book circulation figures, daily attendance averages, numbers of graduates going to colleges and vocational schools, drop-out numbers and causes, instructional supply requests, and countless other factors that may influence learning are necessary for the building administrator.

The Role of the Instructional Leader

The role of the principal in such a school should be to open up channels of communication and free the individual teacher to realize his best abilities. Then the principal should make it possible for the corporate body of teachers to organize so as to meet the school's function, to serve students. But freeing the capacity for the staff to think is not enough.

At no time should the impression be left that the principal isn't responsible, in the final analysis, for the school's policies. To use a committee recommendation as a blind behind which an administrator may hide his own judgment is to mistake the purpose of the advisory committee and to shirk leadership responsibility. Administration is a combination of direction and inspiration. But altogether too much emphasis is placed on the directive function. The pay-dirt of successful administration comes in the supporting role the administrator plays in staff relations.

Before one professional can stimulate another, there must be a free communication based upon warm respect for people and ideas. Such communication takes place when the administrator meets individually and in groups with teachers on both a formal and an informal basis. An atmosphere of respect comes from countless day-to-day major and minor encounters. Getting unusual supplies for class use, rearranging schedules for unusual field trips, listening to bizarre ideas, providing secretarial aid for project assistance—all of these supporting associations of administrator and teacher are part of the effective leader's duty in working with the staff.

The principal must work to bring out the very best in the teaching talent of the staff. He must know the staff members and be aware of the developments in their content fields. The biology teacher, for example, needs to know that the principal too is aware of the National Science Foundation's Biological Science Curriculum Study materials and is anxious to talk over the program. Today's principal must be aware of the content breakthroughs in all areas if he is to be a source of leadership to the modern teaching staff.

The Need for Multidimensional Communication Channels

Decision-making at Lakeview was multidimensional. The matters related to curriculum—determination of course goals, text selection, course requirements and so forth—were the business of the departments, subject to administrative approval. All members of the staff were members of the department in which they taught. It was here that the policy relating to book reporting in English, for instance, was to be discussed. As another example, the teachers of industrial arts developed their own procedures for project activity.

Frequently, recommendations were made by one department to another. For instance, the Social Science Department made a number of suggestions to the Instructional Materials Department on the operation of the library.

Faculty Committees

Each teacher at Lakeview was also a member of a faculty committee. These committees included: policies, professional growth, community and professional communications, research, and social. Composition of these committees was determined by teacher selection, cutting across departmental lines. Here we got views of professionals with different content orientation on common problems. Those who didn't have common interest in curriculum work did have a mutual interest in the policies concerning the broad all-school affairs.

Each of the faculty committees had definite responsibilities. The policies committee, for example, worked on the procedures for the selection and operation of the co-curricular program. The research committee was interested in disseminating research findings, as well as carrying out certain status studies.

The faculty committees served as a communication channel. The faculty committees' leadership rotated each year or so. Matters of any nature were referred to the appropriate faculty committee for study and recommendations by either the principal or a staff member. The committee action was reported at the faculty meeting for final recommendation on policy adoption. The intent of the faculty committee structure was to make it possible for any idea, regardless of where it originated, to receive full and appropriate consideration.

The Department

The school's faculty was divided into departments. The department was organized to bring teachers of related subject disciplines together for coordinating the instructional program and for facilitating program refinement and development in each content area. The departments served as a communication channel to the principal through the weekly meetings of all the department heads with all of the building administrators.

The department head in all Decatur secondary schools was selected by the principal and, in the larger departments, recommended by the superintendent and appointed by the Board of Education. There were department heads in all of the curricular areas in each high school building, and in every case these leaders were responsible for supervision within their departments. They visited classes, held conferences with their teachers on their strengths and weaknesses, made course assignment recommendations and handled early phase budget matters.

The department head was the foundation on which staff progress was built at Lakeview. The department heads met with the principal weekly, meeting to consider over-all problems and to refine procedures to facilitate learning. Individual conferences were held between the principal and the department head to work on specific matters such as the contents of faculty bulletins and the future course of in-service activities.

Without the dedication to the team teaching system and the small and large group organization of the department heads there would not have been the changes which resulted in the Decatur-Lakeview Plan.

The final responsibility rested with the principal for accepting or rejecting changes in policy or procedure on the building level. It is interesting to note that not one suggested policy was rejected in six years at Lakeview! The staff recommendations had been soundly formulated by the time the appropriate group had considered them. No principal worth his salt will allow his headship duties (crowning the homecoming queen, filling in the endless number of forms, purchasing, meetings, etc.) to interfere with his leadership responsibilities. The leadership duties include working with in-service programs, stimulating staff discussions of class problems, studying and disseminating educational research, listening to collective and individual concerns, pointing the way ahead and working to improve the program.

A Two-Way Method of Organization

The two-pronged approach to staff organization used at Lakeview for decision-making was department and faculty committees. It was employed because of the belief that a school's policies were (1) of a specialized nature related to content with specialized interest or (2) of a general nature with universal (or nearly so) application.

The total faculty was not vitally concerned with the reading lists which the homemaking teachers may have felt were important. On the other hand, grading was a concern to the total staff. Thus, the department considered such matters as the homemaking reading lists; the faculty policies committee (one of the faculty committees) worked out possible grading procedures and made recommendations. Another advantage of the dual decision-making system was that it pulled together people of common interest some of the time; at other times it cut across these department lines for the faculty committees and gave a free interchange between members at different departments. On some problems the physical education teachers or the science instructors pooled their points of view and interests to the combined satisfaction of the total faculty.

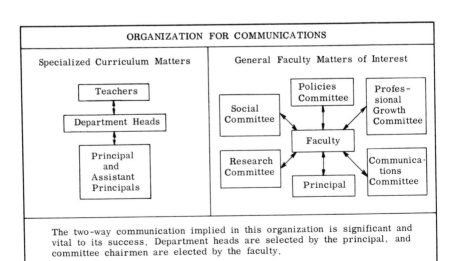

ORGANIZATION FOR COMMUNICATIONS

Specialized Curriculum Matters

General Faculty Matters of Interest

Teachers

Department Heads

Principal and Assistant Principals

Social Committee

Policies Committee

Professional Growth Committee

Faculty

Research Committee

Principal

Communications Committee

The two-way communication implied in this organization is significant and vital to its success. Department heads are selected by the principal, and committee chairmen are elected by the faculty.

The Attitude Toward Meetings

At Lakeview there was a minimum number of meetings scheduled each year for both groups. This doesn't mean there weren't a lot of meetings held each year. Instead it was the practice to be restrictive in the scheduling and permissive in providing the opportunity for added meetings for consideration of pertinent topics. This was done on the theory that there needed to be structure, if any real benefit were to result. Some departments met on a scheduled basis twice a month, while the faculty committees met once each month. A general faculty meeting rounded out the schedule of staff meetings every month. As the department head or committee chairman saw reason for group work, a meeting was called. Some groups met often. The mandate for the extra meetings was the work to be done, not the dictate of a heavy schedule. Staff meetings were so important that as many as possible were scheduled during the regular school day.

The Uses of the Organization

The vehicle for staff participation, though, is of little worth unless it is accepted and respected by all school personnel. Once the structure is established, there needs to be an effort put forth to show by practice that the work which the committees and departments do will be both considered universally and given a fair hearing.

The teacher, first as an individual and then as a group member, is the vital element in any staff formula which seeks program improvement. All of the certified staff are teachers primarily—whether just out of college, whether experienced, whether department head, or whether administrator—and their various roles are contributing to the common group goal: improvement of instruction for each individual student. This equality of purpose does not mean that there is an unanimity of view on almost any topic. On the contrary, it means that in decision formation all are to be heard and considered *in toto* when the final decision must come. To say that administrators should not make decisions and seek united action is to say birds should not fly.

There needs to be a catalyst in the bringing together of worthwhile elements. There is a time for discussion, a time for study, a time for program formulation and a time for action. The person who has the job of administrator and shirks the role does a disservice to his profession. Real unity comes from disciplined diversity.

The Faculty Group as the Source of Action

Group morale is an important matter in any social institution. The wholesome benefits of positive morale are well worth the time and effort which the committees spend. The principal can serve as a tranquilizer, but not as the cure for all problems. The recognition by the organization that the individual is important is essential for the real potential of the group to be realized.

Individuals are important in terms of intrinsic worth, and also (a point sometimes missed), in terms of their role on the staff. The docile conforming personality may be a balance to the aggressive reformer. The negative staff member contributes in his way as much as the yes-man. The teacher who talks out of lack of experience can frequently serve a useful purpose by demonstrating the need for self-regulation to the more experienced staff members. Of course, the individual has to accept corporate responsibilities and obligations for seeing that all is done to work in harmony with the group goals. The administrator must weld the diverse elements into a solid form. This implies a recognition that teachers have one role and administrators another; both are equally important and interdependent.

Chapter
Four

Team Teaching

THERE are almost as many variations of team teaching
as there are applications of the concept, but the common
thread of all these imaginative enterprises is the union of two
or more teachers in a single instructional task. The only defensible motive for team teaching can be improved instruction for students, as a result of bringing the combined talents
of staff together to work on instructional problems.

Some team teaching systems imply the use of paraprofessionals with the certified teachers; others are composed
exclusively of professional staff members. Some cut across
content lines, bringing together teachers of different subject
disciplines; others are composed of teachers from a single
content field. Both vertical and/or horizontal approaches to
subject matter are possible, depending on team composition.

That is, some teams are concerned with a single content area or course; others carry out instruction in more than one content area. Some work with a single grade level, others work with several grade levels. School size and staff interest have a lot to do with the composition of the teaching teams and the election of whom the team will serve. Literature on the subject reports diversity in composition of content and organizational patterns.

Team Teaching in the Decatur-Lakeview Plan

Team teaching at Lakeview was well defined and was, therefore, restricted to a specific meaning for this staff at this particular time. The restrictive elements of the team operational procedures were not meant to be the final word in the use of teaching teams; the definition of team teaching accepted at Lakeview seemed to fit the staff's needs and conformed to the best thinking of the whole faculty at the time of its agreement. As time goes on, the application of team teaching may change. The teams were composed of teachers within a single content area concerned with students on one grade level. While a few teachers were members of more than one team, there was a separate teacher unit or team for each grade level. Great caution was taken to avoid becoming too rigid in the pattern of the structure before its mettle was fully tested. So long as the staff stayed alert and thoughtful, there was reason to assume tomorrow's definition will not be today's!

In some hard-nosed thought sessions in staff meetings and summer workshops, principles and operational procedures were developed and agreed upon. The thought was that a definition to be accepted by everyone was needed before the commonly accepted concept could be tried and tested. If the operational procedure didn't work, then modifications were to be made, but care was taken in adequately testing the functioning of the teams as described. The idea of establishing teams for more than one content area, science and mathematics for ninth grade students for example, was rejected. The staff felt that the teams would be more effective, in the beginning anyway, if the span of content and instructional goals were limited. The point was made that teachers of one content area would have fewer communication problems and would already be commonly oriented. A vision of interdisciplinary teams was not lost, but its implementation didn't seem fruitful for this staff when they were beginning the program.

Lakeview teachers have long had a tradition of cooperative endeavors, though not necessarily working together in instruction. The tradition of the school was one of a great deal of curricular investigation by groups and individuals. Participation in a drop-out study, the common learnings program, the North Central Association's Superior and Talented Student Project and countless other professional concerns had been explored over the years by the staff, independently and sometimes collectively. However, one reality of working with each other on common classroom problems was new. It wasn't long before it was obvious that there was little relationship between working intimately with other teachers and working in isolation on a common problem. The exchange of ideas and the sharing of experience was of far greater value in team effort than in any faculty committee work. There appeared to be a greater desire to come to final, single agreement when a team worked on a concern than when a committee of relatively independent teachers worked on a problem. The agreements the teams made are, however, subject to easier review and change as experience and application test them.

Staff Decisions on Team Teaching

The first decision the staff made, that teaching teams would be within single content areas and that a separate team was to be established for each grade level, was the hardest to make. For owing to the school's size (1,040 students in the six grade levels, 7-12), this meant that some teachers would necessarily be on more than one team since a load could not always be kept on one grade level and in one content area. Furthermore, some requested they not be in only one content area and have membership restricted to one team. Here the necessities of reality and the practicality of satisfying individual teacher preferences were weighed in constructing the teaching assignments. No recommendation for assignments was solicited during the formulation of the guidelines of the Plan. The purpose was to involve staff members in thinking of all roles and procedures without a personal orientation to those they would assume.

Since Lakeview was one of eight secondary schools in a system highly coordinated in organization of content; and since the city-wide curriculum committees set the content guidelines, the arrangement of confining team consideration to the single content area seemed best. The Decatur School District did not regiment content, but did make suggested grade level assignment of general topics.

Team teaching was to be a cooperative venture of professional equals. The concept of the "master" teacher was rejected in favor of the concept of the equality of partners—a decision that deviates from the Trump proposal. Also, responsibility for course planning was shared by all team members. It was agreed, however, that the teacher responsible for the large group presentations was the one who would call the meetings as needed and be responsible to communicate with the department head and administration. Leadership roles within the teams had been developed in an informal but generally recognized way. The role of the members was determined more by group need and interaction than by teaching experience, educational background, tenure at Lakeview, or other individual factors.

Concerns About Teacher Participation
in Team Teaching

In the staff planning workshop a real concern was expressed over the effects of group morale once the decision was reached as to whom the large group teacher would be. After a depth study in the workshop of the role of both large and small group teachers, the administration asked for personal preference recommendations from each teacher. The results were astonishing. Except in one case, the individual election didn't deviate from the administrators' tentative selection. The reason seemed to be that teachers wanted to do what they were good at doing and, conveniently enough, they were good at what they wanted to do; thus the compatibility with the administrative staff assignment decision. Teachers with less teaching experience tended to prefer small group activity. Only unfounded conjecture could isolate the reasons for this.

The teaching team was in every instance assigned the responsibility of:

1. setting course and unit goals;

2. determining evaluation procedures to see if the goals were
   achieved at predetermined bench-mark points in the year;

3. making the learning experience selection in terms of assigned
   reading, necessary reinforcement drill and the like;

4. suggesting resources for students;

5. pooling ideas about the degree of effectiveness of the previously determined large group activities;

6. contributing individual strengths to the team enterprise.

The Lakeview teams had no non-certified personnel assigned to
them. Although there was a need and a place for non-certified workers in the school, the Decatur-Lakeview Plan rejected them as team
members. The use of non-certified workers would be done best
through a pool of secretarial assistance. The teams were not responsible, then, for duplicating materials, for instance, but for constructing
them and making professional decisions. Clerical aid was a distinct
responsibility of the School Service Program, not the teaching teams.

Change in Teacher Behavior Comes After Structured Effort

Cooperative planning was easier said than done. It required an
intellectual honesty and willingness to cooperate which the self-contained classroom organization tended to ignore. Teams that were
immediately successful seemed to be those which started by setting
unit goals and then sought ways to achieve them. Those with more
difficulty in getting organized were those that regarded content to
the exclusion of all else and gave little real consideration to the
process by which students were to learn.

Teachers with a long tenure or those who served as department
heads, in some cases, seemed to be less supple and not as eager to
work with other staff members as the newer staff members. This
problem was the source of a frank discussion in cabinet and faculty

meetings. What was a problem the first year diminished by the third year of the Plan's operation. Over and over the administrators hammered away at the need for full and equal consideration of all ideas from any team member as the standard mode of operation. In one case, a beginning teacher who was somewhat weak in her own beliefs of what should be taught and of how adolescents learn tried to contend that the experienced teachers dominated her thought process. She soon realized, however, that her contention was an excuse, not a reason. Real progress then resulted in the growth of this teacher as a contributing team member; she learned to compensate for her lack of experience by additional study of content and methodology.

A Model Is Given

The model given for faculty discussion was the medical profession with its division of specialization of function and cooperation in consultation. Too frequently, it was thought at first, the educational patient would die while the practitioners were irresolute about the malady and unsure of what the prescription would be. It took time for the teams to develop decision-making procedures and to avoid being bogged down with insignificant planning. By the end of the first month it was evident there was brain-storming on ways to fill voids of understanding among most of the teams. The point is this. The teams made it, some more successfully than others, but all exhibited a tremendous growth in developing areas of specialization by the end of the first year.

In three years at Lakeview three teachers out of a staff of sixty-one were unable to work with others profitably. Interestingly enough, we would say that two shouldn't have been teaching in a traditional instructional program either, for personality characteristics inhibited these people's work with students, as well as teachers. The third was an individual who could have done a good teaching job, as past job performance would indicate, but somehow couldn't tolerate the slightest adult disagreement with her beliefs. We advised such people, and we would advise anyone else who doesn't want to work with other staff members, to accept a teaching position elsewhere. Cold as this may sound, it made sense for both the individuals and for the other faculty members.

Some people were unwilling to accept the suggestions and judgments of other staff members. This, of course, didn't make team teaching a poor enterprise, but it did show another skill teachers need, the ability to work with professional peers. Like other skills, it can be developed and increased or compensated for, but not without effort on the part of administrators and the teachers themselves. Somehow the psychological security of the person is the dimension that sets the bounds of the ability to work with fellow teachers. Teachers who tended to have personality conflicts with other staff members were the ones who were noted for unfortunate incidents with students, it seemed.

Teaching teams took time to jell. There often was the honeymoon period in which all was serene and a division of opinion was not evident; it was even submerged behind stilted agreement and unusual friendliness. Generally, this was because there was little to warrant disagreement. As the teams became more succesfully operative, however, there existed a greater possibility for division of opinion. It was at this point that mutual respect and a clearly defined way of solving differences was necessary. At Lakeview it was agreed that the department chairman was to be the resource person for policy clarification in matters relating to content and methods of instruction, and the principal was the resource person for all other matters. The result was that the department heads were used infrequently and the principal even less in this regard, yet it was understood that an outsider could be called in if the group had a need. Sometimes problem resolution came after emotional conflict.

Eventual results were worth these disruptive experiences since the team came to understand its own structure and thus became more functional and professionally operative. Respect for professional ability has been demonstrated over and over as Lakeview teachers discussed the activities of their teaching teams. The lounge talk frequently centered on a narration of the expert way one teacher handled a situation or worked with an idea. Prior to the team approach little of this knowledge and respect of what others did was noticeable among the staff.

Positive Results of Team Teaching

It was an unproven observation that teachers generally became more interested in their students' progress as the teams became more highly developed. A friendly sense of competition developed among the staff concerning their different small groups. The identification of assignments that didn't help students understand, the recognition of content particularly difficult to students and the other blinds in instructional practice all became more evident when several staff members worked on course design and evaluation. Also, the positive reactions that a good lecture, a vital discussion, or a successful assignment evoked from one's fellow teacher, made the cooperative venture pleasing and stimulating. Understanding and intellectual inquiry often grew quickly within a teaching team.

During the first two years the teams were not scheduled for meetings during the school day. This was a serious error. Team work was too important to be tacked on to the end of the long school day. Therefore, the team members were all assigned common meeting times during the third year. Usually there were three meetings a week. Some teams extended their conferences through dinner together; others met on a rotating basis at each other's home one evening a week. While the husband-teachers worked on solutions to their concerns, the wives socialized during the evening meeting. While no one urged or even suggested these out-of-school team work sessions, the genuine desire to work together and the pleasures that came from it prompted them.

Facilities Influence Staff Activity

The congestion and lack of space in the Lakeview building caused some real difficulty at first. Staff members simply didn't have a place to meet unless it was a hall bench or the front hall ticket booth. The inadequate facilities caused added concern until the problem was rectified. This reinforced the belief that physical facilities are vital. Teams needed a place to meet with resource materials and with equipment and supplies at hand. The surroundings did not need to be lavish but they had to be established, as well as known, and a sense of propriety needed to exist before the limited preparation time became fully useful. No administrator or board of education can afford to overlook the importance of facilities in considering its organization for instruction.

Effective Team Teaching Requires Staff Discussion

The worth of the summer workshops was again pointed out during the third year. During the first two years the workshops were held and the benefits which followed were accepted and taken for granted. The lack of this activity before the third year caused some of the new staff members to be insecure and slower to accept their role of professional equal in team work. A series of after-school coffee sessions was designed to get over this hump. This second-best procedure got across the concept of team teaching, but it took about eight weeks to complete. The workshop the second summer of the Plan's operation did the trick before the first day of instruction! Also, some time was devoted to team teaching considerations in faculty and department meetings.

Numerous conferences between teachers and principal on both an individual and group basis needed to be held to provide a background for new staff members as they became operating members of the teaching team. If our schools cannot or will not reduce teaching loads substantially and if the country really wants improved instruction in the classrooms, the employment of teachers in the summer may be the way to get better instruction for the school year. Talent used in the summer appeared to make teaching talent even more effective during the school year. The Lakeview workshops were the most valuable single factor in developing the Lakeview program.

A beginning teacher wrote at the end of a faculty session on team teaching:

> I like the idea. I can see the advantage of sharing ideas and of giving constructive help to other teachers. This keeps me from getting in a rut. All teachers beginning to work on a team, though, need to understand the students, but we have to try to understand other teachers and, even more important, ourselves.

Team Teaching and Large—Small Group Instruction Aren't the Same

Team teaching is possible in almost any kind of organizational pattern. The small-large group concept doesn't demand team teaching. It would be possible for a single teacher to work with his students in both large and small groups without the cooperation of another teacher. As a matter of fact, this was a necessity in some courses. For example, Lakeview had seventy-two students in first-year Latin. These students were divided in the large-small group pattern with one teacher responsible for both. Although this worked well, the advantages of the team approach, owing to class size, were unfortunately lost.

The Plan implied a reliance on team teaching to realize the fuller advantages of the small and large group program. Also, team teaching brought out the strengths of the various team members. For instance, on one team in English a teacher was talented in art abilities and was able to produce vivid transparencies for use in large groups. In mathematics one teacher had particular skill at test construction and the tests were largely the responsibility of this staff member. The other members of this team worked out suggestions and evaluations to guide this teacher. Somehow there seemed to be a built-in device in teachers who worked closely together in detecting where strengths and weaknesses were in their colleagues; and there was a real desire, altruistically motivated, to be of service and personal assistance to other team members. The value of the support one teacher gave to another teacher on a team shouldn't be overlooked.

The small groups were as diverse in project work and class discussion as the variability of interest and talent of the student membership of each group. No attempt was made to regiment the small group work, for such would be in direct conflict with the goal of individualizing instruction. There was even a rigid conformity to diversity that some observers would question at times. The teams wanted small groups to chew on the concepts presented on the basis of the students' ability. As the group's ability varied, so did the activity and, thus, the progress of the class. The small groups were joined together with common evaluation instruments (whether tests, essays, projects or teacher evaluation of discussion) at the point at which the teacher, as a result of team discussion, felt it was time to move ahead.

Administrative Behavior for Team Teaching

Team teaching did not become effective by the establishment of teams. Its worth was only a reality after cooperative effort was put forth by the various members. Some teams solidified easily; others required either time or direction or both. The administrators needed to make a conscious effort to maintain close contact with what the teams were doing. The administrator's role here was one of a human-relations engineer who listened, asked, proposed, questioned and listened some more. To ignore human relationships, personal attitudes, and individual feelings on and among a staff was to stop the lifeblood of group progress. Teams which did a good piece of work deserved and needed recognition and praise. This came in personal contact as well as in faculty meetings, individual notes, and staff bulletins.

A sense of competition frequently developed on a teaching team and between the teams. This was not petty or negative but was a valuable source of inspiration. The questions of the staff were: Could we work effectively? Could we provide more diverse experiences? Could we harness more beneficial resources? What better use was there of natural competitive traits in teachers?

The essence of team teaching was the freeing of teachers from individual isolated work and bringing them together for their personal stimulation and for joint consideration of common instructional problems. Students profited from this concentration of professional talent in the day-to-day activities in which they were engaged.

Team teaching was more to be noted for its spirit of inquiry and desire to do the very best at each phase of the instructional process than for its organizational pattern. The desire to use everything and everyone, from teaching machines to outside resource people, was characteristic of team teaching. From the down-to-earth planning sessions came the multiple approaches to instruction that produce good instruction. Slumbering talent was called to action as the teams developed new learning experiences for students.

Team teaching may have caused some problems, but they were the kind of problems that inspired better instruction at Lakeview. The isolated classroom concept offered an effective blind for the ineffective principal with a below average teacher who hadn't been given help in improvement. Team teaching, on the other hand, identified teacher deficiency and cried for a solution. Team teaching was an expression of faith in teachers to increase their effectiveness by individual effort in a group enterprise.

Decisions Concerning Team Teaching

A number of decisions needed to be made concerning the team teaching organization at Lakeview. Each consideration of teachers, content, time, group size and composition and facilities required a selection among several alternatives. The chart which follows suggests the dimensions of the considerations. The marked alternatives were the ones employed at Lakeview.

TEAM TEACHING CONSIDERATIONS		
Element	Lakeview Choice	Alternatives
Personnel	* — —	1. Involve members of the existing school staff. 2. Utilize new staff members.
Membership	* — —	1. Two or more professional teachers. 2. Two or more professional teachers with one or more paraprofessional assistants.
Organization	* — —	1. Formal organization with equal status and responsibility of team members. 2. Formal organization with differentiated responsibility and status of team members.

Element	Lakeview Choice	Alternatives
TEAM TEACHING CONSIDERATIONS (continued)		
Organization (continued)		3. Informal organization on an *ad hoc* basis.
Size	* — —	1. Traditional class size of 25-30 students and one teacher—sometimes combined with another group or groups. 2. Varying class size—large groups and small groups.
Group Composition	* — —	1. Random grouping by administrative expedience. 2. Special purpose grouping based on achievement, ability, vocational choice, personality, interest, ethnic group, sex or any other dimension(s). 3. Grouping adjusted on an *ad hoc* basis as the needs of the students require.
Time	* — —	1. Single length class period for all groups at all times. 2. Varying length of class period determined on a prearranged basis. 3. Varying length of class period determined by the purpose of the learning activity on an *ad hoc* basis.
Schedule	* — —	1. Daily cycle. 2. Multiple day cycle. 3. Week cycle. 4. Open-ended cycle.
Content	* — —	1. Single subject area with specified content. 2. Two or more subject areas with specified content.

TEAM TEACHING CONSIDERATIONS (continued)		
Element	*Lakeview Choice*	*Alternatives*
Content (continued)		3. Single subject area with unspecified content. 4. Two or more subject areas with unspecified content.
Facilities	* — —	1. Utilize existing facilities. 2. Rearrange and/or redeploy existing facilities. 3. Construct new facilities.

Chapter
Five

*The Division
of the School Day
and the School Week*

EDUCATORS have long recognized the desirability of
structuring a school day in diverse ways. A review of the
organizational pattern of secondary schools attests to the lack
of agreement on any single best organization for instruction.
Some schools use forty-minute periods, others employ fifty-
to sixty-minute class periods. No evidence has been presented
which would conclude that one pattern is better than another
for maximum student achievement. The fault with all schedules
involving single length periods is that they don't allow for
diverse use of time to the advantage of students. The school
day should be organized in a way that gives the learning activities requirements the time proportionment; the school day
should not, as is the usual case, impose a rigid time structure
upon content.

The variation among school activities is partially determined by the organization of the school day. For example, a school with a five-period day allows students to be in five groups each day or in twenty-five each week. The greater the number of periods of time in the day and week, the more different groups and scheduling possibilities there are.

Much is being written in the journals about scheduling as related to unstructured schedules or totally flexible schedules. Some of this is confusing and unrealistic, we believe. A school of seventy staff members and a thousand students needs some organizational form before it can be sensibly managed. The procedure of bringing students and teachers together on a different schedule each day of the school year, and some advocate this, may have some merit. But actually to accomplish this would dissipate too much time and energy, even if it were valuable educationally. Furthermore, a schedule isn't a schedule if it is truly flexible. That is, if a single teacher or team of teachers can alter time requirements substantially on an *ad hoc* basis for a given day, there isn't a consistent pattern to guide other staff and to stabilize the time students have for independent or outside study.

Somehow, the staff felt if the small and large group pattern was to be effectively used there had to be a compromise between the rigid seven-periods-a-day traditional schedule Lakeview had previously used and a complete lack of structure.

Time Became a Variable

In considering the matter of organizing the school day, the staff agreed that some activities required more class time than others. The clothing teacher, for example, wanted her students to have a two-hour laboratory period in order to allow students to find a sense of completion and satisfaction in a given task. It would, she argued, allow for more trial-and-error in learning how to construct clothing. This homemaking instructor felt it was wise to economize the starting and stopping time and thus to increase the actual work time for each student. She calculated that in the traditional schedule seven minutes were lost each day the class met, four minutes at the beginning and three minutes at the end of most periods in dismissal and storage of materials and equipment. While the same amount of preparation for work and storage time was still consumed in the two-hour classes, this time was lost only half as often because the course met for a longer duration. The other teachers of laboratory courses agreed.

After staff study it was agreed that various learning activities require different amounts of time. Also, it was concluded that some subjects demand daily meetings while others do not. It was thought that those subjects which emphasize attitude formation and skill development required more student class time over an extended period than those which are more knowledge-oriented.

Class Size Becomes a Variable

The faculty saw the sense of varying group sizes for varying instructional experiences. They saw merit in bringing a number of students together for a lecture and then organizing small discussion groups to evaluate the lecture content. In such groups students could express the knowledge gained in both lecture and outside reading. The principle agreed upon was this: The nature of the learning activity should determine the group size. This principle was found to have application in all content areas and on all grade levels.

Once the staff agreed it was appropriate for students to meet in groups of varying size for different purposes, it was also agreed that the length of these meetings should vary. Some teachers wanted students to meet in a large group and a small group on the same day; others saw advantage for their students to have daily contact with the content, but in different-sized groups. Therefore, a schedule was needed at Lakeview that opened many alternatives, depending on the needs of students and the nature of the course.

Fifteen Building Blocks in Each Day

To make it possible for more groups to meet and to allow for a difference in the duration of class time for various groups, the day at Lakeview was divided into fifteen twenty-seven minute periods. Beginning school at 8:10 A.M. and ending at 3:46 P.M. allowed the day to be broken into one ten-minute announcement period and fifteen instruction periods. Some learning groups met for one period (module), others met for the equivalent of two to six periods each time they met. Whenever a class was desired which was to last more than a half-hour, it was organized by combining two or more periods into a coordinated block of time. The flexibility in the Decatur-Lakeview Plan was one result of the various time combinations possible in the fifteen-period schedule.

The Lakeview day was divided into periods of twenty-seven minutes because it was believed that this is the appropriate length of time for the shortest profitable activity, the large group class.

The belief that lectures should be limited in duration has been confirmed by experience at Lakeview that an adolescent profits more from a twenty-seven minute lecture than from a longer lecture. If a teacher feels a class needs more than one lecture a day, we say fine; but no single lecture should be more than twenty-seven minutes long. The staff has observed schools using fifty-minute and forty-minute lecture periods and has judged the effectiveness as far as the student is concerned to be greater with a twenty-seven minute lecture. Some experimentation was carried on at Lakeview to develop techniques of instruction for large groups involving a double session of fifty-seven minutes. Included in these sessions were the use of work sheets, group discussion from the floor, panels, and homework time followed by the teacher giving some answers. These were in addition to the regular lecture. Since the prospects did not look bright for this kind of activity from the beginning, it was abandoned and all teachers at Lakeview were restricted to the half-hour duration.

Once a teacher had taxed a student's attention span, the effectiveness of the presentation was diminished. We contend there is no reason to give a lecture unless it is effective for the student, regardless of how good a long narration makes the teacher feel. Even within this twenty-seven minute lecture, it was recommended that the teacher vary the pace about three times by the use of filmstrips, overhead transparencies, work sheets, humor or some other device. Good lecturers soon developed the skill to make the point and move ahead.

Single Module Lectures Work Well

Contrary to the first thought of some of the visitors to the Lakeview building, the twenty-seven minute lecture worked as well with the seventh as with the twelfth grade students. It was noticed that as students were in the program for several years, as they moved from the seventh to the upper grades, they became very effective at note-taking, fact-sorting and idea-grasping.

Up to two hundred students were in a single lecture class. More could have been involved if the student body were larger. The number of students in the lecture—whether two hundred or fifty—didn't have any noticeable effects on student or teacher reactions. After all, the transmission of ideas from teacher to student in a lecture is highly individualized as far as the receiver, the student, is concerned. The number of students, whether great or small, who listen at the same time doesn't influence the individual learner's understanding. The communication is on a single line, from teacher to student. The goal is to get the best possible presentation of ideas to each student, irrespective of the size of the group in which the communication takes place.

The Week Was the Scheduling Unit

The staff agreed, as has been previously mentioned, that it was folly to assume that all subjects require equal time. Therefore, varying lengths of time per day and per week were spent on the different subjects. For purposes of scheduling, the week was designated as the basic time unit. The schedule for each day can vary but the schedule for each week—for a semester at least—is constant. In the traditional schedule the basic unit is often the day, with each day organized identically or substantially the same as each other day. In the Decatur-Lakeview Plan schedule the week is the unit, calling for different activities each session or network of related sessions for a week.

Once an agreement was reached on the week as the basic unit of class meeting and the session (module) of twenty-seven minutes the division, the next step was to consider the distribution of the sessions for each course on each grade level.

As in all aspects of this program, this was done through staff participation. Every department was asked to work out an ideal time distribution for each course. The change was made to develop the best recommendation (1) of group composition, whether large, medium or small; (2) of number of meetings in each group per week per course; and (3) of the amount of independent study time desired. Every force was put behind throwing off the shackles of previous time distribution practices. The only consideration was what was best—in terms of effective and efficient use of student time—for students to master the course goals.

The consideration given this concern by the staff was deliberate, penetrating and diverse. The time distribution varied between departments and within departments. The competence of the staff was evident once again when the recommendations of one curricular area were made which were not equal or similar to those of other areas. Contrary to the prediction of a seasoned, perhaps too much so, administrator, the teachers did not try to claim a disproportionate amount of time for their content area. All worked out the time and group size needs which they thought were ideal. Teachers knew the inadequacies or overabundance of time for their courses. The job was to involve all the staff in the consideration of their courses. They sensed where students needed concentration, in listening to presentation, in practicing or doing and in having teacher supervision. Some staff members felt that less time in class meant it was better to have smaller classes. Such was the case in auto mechanics. The teacher thought it better to have shorter class time but to have more independent study time for students to work on their own and smaller classes for closer teacher-student contact.

Another interesting outcome of the staff study was the desire in all content areas to keep certain principles of time distribution in mind in making these decisions. These principles were:

1. Students profit from being in groups of varying size within the same courses.

2. Students generally can master various courses in different amounts of time.

3. Individual or independent study time is a part of the pattern of instruction in all courses.

4. The recommendation for time and group size is determined by student need, not teacher preference.

Course Specifications Vary

During this staff discussion period the center of interest was on the students' schedule and not the teachers'. Too often the length of a course and the frequency of meetings is predicted on how long the teacher feels a need to teach, not how long it takes a student to learn. The harness of tradition keeps many educators from re-examining the distribution of time in the school day, week or year.

Once all these recommendations were made to the department head by each teacher or teachers of a course, they were submitted to the building administrators. A number of trial schedules were made for students with various ability and vocational profiles. These showed the amount of time students would be in class each week. They were sent back to the departments and discussed in building meetings. In no case were the recommendations unacceptable in terms of staff availability or student workability. However, adjustments were made, with some students being given more independent study time. During the first year there was a tendency for there to be fewer lectures than in succeeding years. Correspondingly, fewer hours were suggested for individual or independent study time the first year of the Plan's operation than later in its development. This suggests some success at meeting the goal of the program of increased student responsibility for learning. Also, it implies added staff effectiveness in motivating students for this dimension of learning. Lakeview students began doing more work on their own.

Each year reconsideration was given to the number of the various groups per week for each course. Wisdom was not achieved during the first consideration of the topic, nor were the needs of all students isolated in an absolute manner. Adjustment and alteration were always necessary if the sharp edges were to be refined into a smooth program and if the changing character of the student population was to be considered.

Generally speaking, Lakeview students spent fifty per cent of their time in small groups, twenty per cent of their school day in large groups and thirty per cent of their school hours in independent study. The staff would like to have had the independent study time increased and the small group time decreased. At one juncture, such did not seem in the students' best interests. Lakeview students needed the small group time and profited from the existing amount of large group instruction.

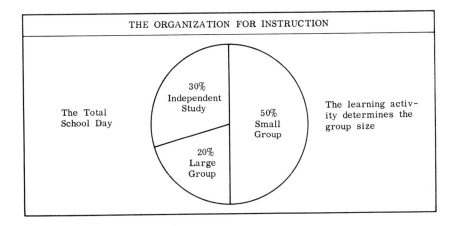

Independent Study—Group Size: Varies from 1 to 60 students.

FUNCTIONS:

1. Develop creative and independent thought
   (through producing and "doing")
2. Strengthen background knowledge
   (through special reading, outlining, etc.)
3. Increase special talents
   (through concentrated effort)
4. Enlarge capacity for self-development
   (through personal responsibility for learning)

Small Group Instruction—Group Size: 5 to 15 students.

FUNCTIONS:

1. Discuss content presentation
   (by student involvement)
2. Strengthen basic skills
   (by speaking, writing, reading)

   3. Promote group activity
      (by shared experiences—panels, buzz groups, etc.)
   4. Add to personal development
      (by frequent class participation)
   5. Increase individualized instruction
      (by added teacher attention)

Large Group Instruction—Group Size: 50 to 220 students.

FUNCTIONS:

   1. Introduction of topics
      (with reasons for learning)
   2. Development of background
      (with coordination of previous knowledge)
   3. Presentation of content
      (with development of generalizations)
   4. Enrichment of instruction
      (with films, recordings, resource experts, etc.)
   5. Evaluation of achievement
      (with testing, written idea development, etc.)

The Teacher's Day Varies

In the traditional seven-period day, Lakeview teachers had five periods each day of teaching assignment, whether class, study or supervision (in the case of department heads). In addition, each had two periods of preparation each day. One day was like all others with little variability in the schedule from day to day. Under the Decatur-Lakeview Plan, however, the schedule for teachers varied from day-to-day, although each day of the week was like all corresponding days of the month. For instance, Monday's schedule was the same throughout the month, but it was likely to be different from that of Tuesday and the other days of the week. Instead of contact hours with students each week, this determination of the teacher's load was made in relation to the specific teaching assignment.

A formula for allocating time for teaching and preparation was arrived at in the belief that all members of the staff needed time to prepare for their instruction. In addition, team membership meant that increased time was necessary for the professional activity implied herein. The commitment to team teaching would be a shallow principle without adequate preparation or meeting time.

While we would like to have had even more time for preparation for all the staff, the practical reality of an acceptable ratio of teachers to students dictated the formula accepted. It was difficult to do minute preparation for small groups. What students said and questioned, of course, defied prior planning, but the small group teacher needed time for reading, for studying, for paper correction and for work in the Instructional Materials Center.

Teachers who were team members often spent more time in team meetings than the schedule dictated; therefore, in addition to designated team meeting times, an attempt was made in the schedule construction process to program team members together as much as possible for their non-student content planning time. Also, team members were scheduled for common lunch hours when possible.

The amount of preparation time, when the formula was applied to all the staff, varied considerably. Teachers presenting content in two areas usually had twice the preparation time of the teacher leaders. We have concluded that the non-contact time teachers spent during the school week was productive and important in affecting the quality of instruction which went on in the varying sized classes.

A home base office was provided for each teacher. Usually it was in a room with other members of the team and always with other members of the same department. The offices were clustered around the Instructional Materials Center, bringing teachers, materials and, it was hoped, students together as the need mutually existed. The point was this: There was a great deal of student contact in one-to-one and small informal group situations during the preparation time. It was not at all unusual to see teachers working with students in their independent study time. Such was not a prevalent practice prior to the Decatur-Lakeview Plan. It was, however, once the Plan was in operation.

The teacher's day varied, then, according to his instructional assignment; and the student's program also was different each day of the week. The individualized program constructed for each student, depending on his instructional needs, was fitted into the seventy blocks of time which constituted the week, as opposed to a weekly schedule of seven periods duplicated each day of the week.

Chapter
Six

The Construction
of the Master Schedule

THERE are few operations in a school as important as the determination of the school's master schedule. The master schedule organizes the potential use of all of the school's talent —both teachers and students—and time. The schedule gives no guarantee of results; only the people involved can affect the results. A schedule constructed without rational planning inhibits teachers' talents.

Too often school principals give scant attention to this critical leadership responsibility. It is easier to adapt last year's schedule to next year's student enrollment than to begin anew in the laborious and time-consuming effort of constructing a new schedule. Also, the day-to-day pressures of the high school principalship frequently necessitate expediency. Such haste often results in construction of the master schedule being postponed until the late summer flurry of activity. School boards some-times obstruct administrative planning by deferring decisions on bud-gets and personnel until the summer months. The construction of the master schedule deserves expert attention and requires a concentrated chunk of time. Since much of what goes on in a school is influenced by the master schedule, it should rank high on the list of functions performed by the building administrators.

Decisions to Be Made for the Master Schedule

The master schedule is the device used to bring students into con-tact with content and teachers. How this is done has a great influence on the quality of the educational experiences a school can offer. Rational choice must be exercised on some basic alternatives. First, a decision needs to be made as to how much the student's day is to be structured. That is, are students to be scheduled in class groups all or a designated segment of the day? Concurrently a decision needs to be made as to how often classes shall meet each day or week. Second, the kinds of learning groups must be defined; that is, content and student must be made compatible on the basis of ability, achievement, maturation, etc. Third, teacher capabilities must be assessed and assigned. Before a teacher is given a professional job to do with a learning group, the responsible authority should decide where and how teaching time should be employed. If all teachers don't do all functions of the teach-ing task equally well, then they should be assigned to do those things they can do best.

The Attitude of Regulating Agencies
Concerning Experimentation

Legal requirements for distribution of time and frequency of class meetings must be honored, but it is significant to note the trend away from requiring equal time and daily meetings for all subjects. State departments of instruction and accrediting agencies are moving away from insisting on rigid specifics in these matters. Instead, they are en-couraging carefully planned experimental deviations. The North Cen-tral Association of Colleges and Secondary Schools actively encourages innovation and experimentation, contrary to the beliefs of some.

Variations Possible in the Use of Time

The Decatur-Lakeview Plan demonstrated that it is folly to assume that it takes the same amount of pupil-teacher contact to learn to type as to learn a foreign language. Some courses required daily formal class meetings and others did not. There was not reason to assume, for instance, that students profited from a daily meeting in industrial arts more than in a meeting of extended length two or three times a week. A course in Spanish, for example, needed to meet each day to strengthen the development of the listening and speaking skills of the language, for here the frequent exposure to the content was a stimulant to progress. The length of classes in Spanish varied on different days of the week, though, depending on the teacher's purpose for the daily meeting. Sometimes all Spanish students met to hear a lecture or see a film, sometimes one class met in the language laboratory, and at still another time a different class would meet in small groups for discussion. In the industrial arts class the benefits of increased laboratory time contributed to increased skill development over the shorter daily periods. When the class met, the meeting time was long enough to get some work done in detail.

As the staff considered the length of time needed for mastery of a course, they also had to consider the kind of instructional groups needed in each course. Those activities which did not require student interaction were to go on in a large group. Those activities of a course which needed fewer students in the learning situation were to go on in small groups. Finally, those activities which were carried on individually and did not need direct teacher supervision were to go on in independent study.

Research studies on various lengths of time for high school subjects have given no clue that the time distribution is the critical element in the quality of learning which results. Of far greater influence on learning than the arrangement of time are the use of human resources, teachers and students.

As the staff considered the amount of time and the size of the learning group, some worthwhile things happened. Teachers became introspective and exercised critical value judgments about how they taught and how students learned. It was not uncommon for instructors to censure themselves for excessive lecturing. Frequently they decided to give more attention to working with students, as opposed to talking to them.

The staff should be involved in the development of the master schedule. They should make recommendations on course time and group specifications. Who is in a better position to make these decisions than the people who are actually going to carry out their results? Each Lakeview department gave these matters serious consideration and submitted recommendations on courses to be offered, on number of students in the various groups, and on the length of time that each group should meet.

The Distribution of Time

At Lakeview it was decided, for the reasons already mentioned, that classes would meet for varying lengths of time. For purposes of schedule construction the length of the shortest class was the block or module used in dividing the school day into assigned segments or building blocks. Fifteen modules of twenty-seven minutes comprised the school day. When longer sessions were wanted, two, three or more consecutive modules were combined.

While other blocks of smaller or larger duration could have been used, it was decided that the instructional procedures would be built on modules of this length. The final decision about the amount of time for each course was made by the principal, but the decision was based on the recommendation of the teaching staff.

The fundamental assumptions made in a varying class size, and irregular meeting time schedule are given below.

Principle:	Students learn at different rates.
Implication:	Classes between and in a course should meet for varying amounts of time.
Principle:	The instructional process is one in which students are sometimes quasi-active (listening) and sometimes personally active (doing).

Implication:	Sometimes students should meet in large groups and sometimes in small groups. The learning activity purpose should determine the group size.
Principle:	Students assimilate ideas and improve skills through their own work. Learning is an active process.
Implication:	Time should be set aside for students to be engaged in productive aspects of learning, for independent study. Students should be free to work on their own.
Principle:	Teachers have talents which vary with the different functions of the teaching process.
Implication:	Some teachers should work with large groups in presenting ideas and others should work with small groups in student-centered work. The special abilities of the teacher should be considered in making teaching assignments.

Learning Groups Should Have Specifications

The composition of the learning groups has received too little attention in most schools. While it is true that ability and/or achievement grouping comes in and goes out of vogue, the attention of educators has not been spotlighted enough on the specifications of learning groups. This is unfortunate. The students in any group can support and stimulate one another.

At Lakeview each department was asked to submit recommendations on the similar qualities it wanted students to have for the various learning groups. Some areas wanted achievement grouping, others wanted ability grouping. Still others sought to bring students with the same emotional characteristics together or to group youngsters by sex. Vocational choice, ethnic background and countless other possibilities of organizing students into a permissive atmosphere for learning were considered and employed. Favorable results were achieved by this new emphasis on group composition.

No group specification was worth anything unless the instructional procedures were adapted to the group's needs. For example, ability grouping was only beneficial if the teachers regulated the content and adjusted the activities to meet the particular needs of the students who comprised the group. There were no particular advantages in grouping the high-ability United States history students if they weren't to use different materials and carry on depth studies. The group itself wasn't a positive force for improvement until the teacher shaped the work to meet the group's interests and abilities.

Talents of Teachers Are a Vital Consideration

Once the ingredients for the instructional program were selected —the content, the time, the group composition—consideration was given to choice of teacher. This too was a valuable kind of consideration for teachers to engage in on a department basis. It caused them to assess their strengths and, in some cases, to realign their teaching practices.

Once staff members began to think about differences among students, the school became a better place to help individual students. The determination of the group specification standards resulted in provisions in learning experience selection and teaching procedures to be made. If the teachers were a part of the decision-making process in this regard, the administrators felt, the chances of successful practice were increased.

The experience at Lakeview revealed that teachers generally elected the kind of group, large or small, that the administrators would select for them. Somehow teachers liked to do those things which they did well and rejected the role in which they were not competent. Department heads made their assessments of the teachers' recommendations in a conference with the principal. The Lakeview administrators knew far more about the staff after these conferences than they learned by class visits and individual conferences.

Some teachers did a splendid job of organizing materials and of presenting them in an interesting and dynamic fashion. Others did not. These teachers tended to be child-centered and liked youngsters more than they enjoyed the content itself. They got their satisfaction from informal face-to-face meetings on an *ad hoc* basis and were interested in content only incidentally. Such teachers were assigned to work with small groups and to assist students in independent study. This does not mean they were not competent in their subject field, but it meant they gained more personal enjoyment from working with people than with ideas alone. The consideration of teacher talent was a major part of the construction of the master schedule.

The best use of teacher capabilities is perhaps the primary consideration in assembling the master schedule. Teaching becomes a satisfaction of a passion as well as a job. To ignore the differences among a teaching staff is to lose sight of a great wealth of instructional potential.

The Mechanics of Scheduling

Once the educational decisions about the schedule were made, the various pieces had to be combined into a coordinated whole. This was a time-consuming and laborious task. Though the last word hasn't been said on schedule construction, there are some procedures which experience has proven effective in constructing the master schedule for a small and large group program.

The schools will benefit appreciably when more attention is given to ways to make creative innovations functional. Data processing procedures and systems analysis studies hold promise for the future of schedule construction. At present the construction of the master schedule is a tedious, tiresome job. While data processing will sort students into classes, it will not produce the master schedule, though this too will probably be solved in the near future. The time will come when an administrator can reserve his time for thinking about imaginative teaching-learning possibilities and make decisions on the best use of staff talent. The powers of data processing will translate these goals into a workable combination of time and talent. For the time being we must content ourselves with only the use of the mind and its memory in constructing the schedule.

While the staff was studying and deciding the kinds of groups, the number of meetings, and the length of sessions for each course, students were making their tentative course elections. The tentative elections served as a tool for the counselors in educational planning with students and gave the administration an estimate of the numbers to be accommodated in each course. Student election of courses and staff decisions in learning group specifications must be made before the mechanics of scheduling can be done, but they are unrelated operations.

Once the staff decisions were made and the tentative election tallies were completed, the mechanics of scheduling began.

STEPS IN MASTER SCHEDULE GENERATION
1. List all courses and designate whether they are to meet in small, medium or large groups.
↓
2. Determine the number of sections for each course.
↓
3. Put all single section large group classes on the master schedule first.
↓
4. Arrange the large group classes for each grade level so they meet during the same module but on different days whenever possible.
↓
5. Assign all single section small group classes to hours which do not conflict with the large groups.
↓
6. Put all multiple section small groups on the master schedule.
↓
7. Assign teachers to the various learning groups.

A great deal of adjusting and readjusting had to be made as each piece of the schedule puzzle was manipulated to fit in place.

Added difficulty and increased time consumption took place whenever the sequence listed above was not followed.

The number of sections was determined by comparing the number of teacher hours available for instruction and the number of students to be put in each section. This analysis indicated to the administrator the number of teachers needed in each department and for every course. Appendix III gives a tabulation of this sort. Also, a comparison is made in this appendix of the course needs and teacher load if the school would be organized on a traditional schedule and of the course needs and teacher load if the Decatur-Lakeview Plan was used.

The value in putting the large group single sections on the schedule first was that it was easier to move small groups than large groups. Since there were only two large group instructional areas available at Lakeview, the large groups had to be scheduled so that no more than two met at one time. The lack of facilities was compensated for by use of a scheduling check-list form which accounts for rooms on the left side and the modules on the top of the form. A separate check sheet was needed for each day of the week since facilities had a different use each day.

Care was taken to make certain that no student would have consecutive large group classes so that students would have a relief from concentrated doses of large groups. Perhaps this wasn't worth the effort, for the break of three minutes after each large group class and the beginning of thought on a different subject by another teacher's direction might have been sufficient to relieve a student's attention span.

There was merit in putting the large groups for all the students of one grade level in the same module on different days, for this helped when the copying of schedules was to be done. A more important reason for this is that it made it possible for teachers to exchange modules when the need arose. For instance, one teacher may need more lecture time on a Monday when a lecture isn't normally scheduled and another may not have the demand for this time, even though Monday is set aside for the large group. Though Lakeview teachers did not exchange modules regularly, they could when they wanted to do so; and there was a positive value served in being able to do so. Once again the belief in a need for flexibility in scheduling applied to the school's daily operation.

The assignment of the small group classes to the master schedule required concentration and the willingness to check and recheck the assignments previously made. Care had to be taken to avoid conflict with another class a student was liable to elect or be placed in by virtue of the grouping specifications. For instance, English-accelerated small groups needed to be put on the master schedule at a time when other courses these students would elect would not meet.

Once the single section small groups were put in place, the multiple sections were added. It was moving these sections that made the balancing of classes taught at various times in the day possible. It was good to keep in mind an idea about the number of section meetings at a given time. By keeping the total number of sections under consideration, the independent study facilities weren't overtaxed at any given time. There would have been no sense in freeing students for independent study if the facilities weren't available.

Finally, the teaching assignments were made. These, as stated previously, were based on the teacher's selection, the department head's recommendation and the principal's approval. Sometimes the small groups needed readjustment to fit the available time teachers had for instruction. This was a minor problem and required no drastic revisions, although it too was time-consuming.

Staff Review of Schedule

Once the first draft of the master schedule was completed, it was given to the staff for criticism and recommendation. Curiously enough, at this stage a number of adjustments were recommended by the staff, for somehow the time lapse between the first recommendations and the tentative draft resulted in a number of desired changes. These were usually easy to satisfy. When all the recommendations were made and all the teacher comments were evaluated by the principal, the final schedule was established and published.

Now the time-consuming secretarial work began. The office

workers, under the supervision of the assistant principal, matched the student elections with the master schedule. This netted a number of conflicts which required some additional adjustment of the master schedule.

The principle was accepted at Lakeview that no student should be kept out of a course he wanted because of the arrangement of the master schedule. The scheduling, an administrative device, should conform to student needs. The student should not have to make elections based on a predetermined master schedule, but on what seemed most to his educational advantage. The limitation of facilities in some areas, particularly industrial arts and science, caused this principle to be disregarded, however. No schedule could be devised to counteract inadequate and insufficient facilities.

The assistant principal moved nine small groups, comprising fifty-three students, to enroll an eighth grade girl in an accelerated algebra class. This operation took over twenty hours. He was vexed when it was learned that she was moving to another school. In spite of such experiences as this, administrators' and teachers' time was not spared in arranging the master schedule to fit the students' instructional needs.

The Schedule Construction Timetable

A timetable was set up for the construction of the master schedule. By working on the schedule over an extended period, each step was given serious consideration and all the staff could deliberate on its construction. The timetable was:

October —Teachers establish courses and grouping specifications.

November—Teachers recommend the number of large and small groups for each course.

December —Principal submits the tentative schedule of large group classes to faculty for criticism.

January —Tentative elections of courses come in from students.

February	—Principal submits the tentative schedule of small group classes to the faculty for criticism.
March	—Tentative assignment of students to sections begins.
June-September	—Adjustments and changes are made as students alter their goals and as teacher recommendations change.

A schedule such as the one used in the Decatur-Lakeview Plan is not developed without the cooperation of the teaching staff. Schedule construction for September of one year must begin in October of the preceding year. As one discusses *how* students will learn, it is necessary to consider *what* students will be exposed to in each course. No staff considerations are more important than the *how* and *what* of the school.

Part
Two

A Technology
and a New Structure
for Learning

True greatness is the most ready to recognize and most willing to obey those simple outward laws which have been sanctioned by the experience of mankind, and we suspect the originality which cannot move except on novel paths.

J. A. Froude

Chapter
Seven

Multimedia Aids
and Programmed Learning
Fit in the Plan

S CHOOL people have given scant attention to the possibilities of improving instruction by the use of multimedia teaching aids. Though the wonders of machines and
materials have contributed to modern man's advance in almost every area of endeavor, their use in the schools is drastically limited.

The past is too much with us in instructional methodology.
We teach as we were taught. Little improvement has taken
place in our methods of instruction. The result is that the lion's
portion of the instruction is given verbally.

Multimedia teaching aids available to teachers today include electronic and video tapes, transparencies for use on
overhead projectors, films and film strips, disk recordings,
mock-ups, television, flannel board materials, learning pro-

grams, printed materials of all kinds and charts, in addition to chalk boards. Hundreds of commercially prepared sets of teaching aids can be purchased which are compatible with most text materials. Many teachers like to prepare their own teaching aids, and the supplies and materials to do so are being produced in such a way that they are easy and relatively economical to use. One of the contributing functions of the paraprofessional worker is to construct teaching aids as needed by the teaching staff.

The Chalk Board, Old but Effective

The chalk board is a good instructional aid. It provides the opportunity for learners to see what teachers are saying. Thus, a second sense, sight, is called into play in the learner to support the audio image the mind pictures as the teacher presents ideas or facts. Too little consideration is sometimes given to the manner in which an appeal is made to the learner. Teachers who fail to use every possible communication channel do their students an injustice. The more approaches used in instruction, the greater the probability of success in dealing with a diverse group of learners. The break in pace and the visual presentation the chalk board or any teaching aid allows is better than word-upon-word lectures.

During a discussion the chalk board is at hand to give a quick, accessible means of visualizing important ideas. Students, as well as teachers, should feel free to use it as a means of facilitating communication in a learning group. Students in the small groups at Lakeview used the chalk board frequently.

Lakeview teachers used the magnetic chalk board effectively in driver education and in science. In driver education model cars were moved in the lanes put on the board, and in science the planets of the universe were rotated around the sun in illustration of planetary motion. Teachers in both subjects found it easy for students to understand the principles they were teaching with the help of the visual movable objects on the magnetic chalk board.

A Needed Trend With Teaching Aids

The current introduction of newer media for instruction, overhead projectors and disks, is not the first revolution in method of content presentation. Erasmus saw the printed page as a bold new way of communicating ideas. It is interesting to note how accurately Erasmus predicted the increase in idea transmission as the result of the printed word. Before the use of movable type by Gutenberg, c. 1456, learning was essentially an auditory process. Students learned by listening and by reciting. Once movable type came into use, the stream of thinking was released by this new medium, the printed page. We are living in a time when the introduction of video-taped materials, electronic tapes, overhead transparencies and other teaching aids will revolutionize the method of instruction, almost as much as the printed page did for the schools of the Middle Ages.

Today's teacher should be aware of the tremendous possibilities for learning in the employment of multimedia teaching aids. The teaching aids are all junior partners to the successful teacher. The job of successful instruction is to overcome barriers to learning. Daydreaming, discomfort and lack of interest make it difficult for the instructor's message to be received by the learner. The multimedia aids are attention-getters, mind-stimulators, thought-provokers. The "large group" teachers at Lakeview were generous in using these aids in their content presentations.

Aids Help Students Conceptualize Knowledge

The basis of understanding for any learner is his own previous experience. The teaching aids help the student form attitudes and crystallize ideas by showing the relationship of what the student hears and what he sees. The only limits on learning should be the student's interest and his capacity to learn. All other obstacles of knowing can be eliminated by well-prepared appeals to the learners' senses of hearing, seeing and feeling. To select and produce these teaching aids is to put an additional claim on teachers' time. Some compensation needs to be made, then, in the class-scheduling process. This is another reason for flexible scheduling and team teaching. It gives some teachers time to prepare multimedia teaching aids. Also, school boards should consider the employment of technicians who will assist teachers in locating and producing appropriate materials.

Selection of teaching aids was an important concern for the teaching teams at Lakeview. The contributions the various members of the teams made to one another was outstanding in finding appropriate teaching aids. Often the small group teachers would make suggestions to the large group teacher as to how a specific visual presentation might clarify a difficult point.

Students used the teaching aids in their independent study. A review of an overlay on a transparency, a rerun of a lecture tape, or a filmed explanation sometimes helped students add to their knowledge of the topic under consideration. Students profited from using each aid in the manner they saw fit. Some needed only casual use, others required prolonged attention to the learning aid.

More Is Needed in the Curriculum

Perhaps the generation of youngsters in our schools today are the first of men who are no longer earth bound. Certainly the trip in space made by Astronaut Gordon Cooper, for example, and the other events in space exploration mean we must have an instructional system which encompasses the consideration of the mysteries of the universe outside our planet. Only audiovisual aids can appropriately present these latest adventures of man to the students. Data-gathering machines have been where man hasn't. The video films and prototype models of space age developments should be a part of every American high school.

This is not to say we can afford to exclude the wisdom of the ages, but we must require that we teach more in our schools today than we did even a decade ago. To get everything included in a curriculum that students need, we must be selective and efficient in what we teach. Programmed instruction, television, films, tapes and other teaching aids will help us in becoming more efficient and competent, giving youngsters the exposure to ideas they need for living in tomorrow's world.

Boards of education that want quality instructional programs will do well to consider the possibility of achieving their goal by employing staff during the summer to select and prepare effective learning aids for use during the regular school year. It makes more sense financially to employ a teacher for an additional one-ninth salary than to reduce the teacher load by one-fifth (one class ordinarily) to produce multimedia aids. The Lakeview summer workshops proved to be valuable in the development of the Decatur-Lakeview Plan.

Lakeview Teachers Focused Attention on Teaching Aids

Lakeview teachers really concentrated on using the multimedia teaching aids in their instruction. This staff's use of the teaching aids had some pronounced influence on the school budget. Language laboratories, thousands of transparency sheets, hundreds of film strips and the equipment to use them all cost money and a lot of it. Quality instruction cannot ever be inexpensive. The evaluation by all concerned was that the money spent on teaching aids was well spent.

Sometimes at Lakeview the use of the teaching aids was slow in coming, even after a large expenditure was made. There was often a lag between our commitment to an idea and our adoption of it in practice. A few teachers selected machines and materials they later did not use, usually because of lack of experience at employing these aids.

To break down the resistance to using the teaching aids several approaches were used. Faculty bulletins hit hard at the advantages of using each specific aid. Concrete examples were given of the use of each piece of equipment. For example, one bulletin cited the splendid use made in one English small group class of the opaque projector in teaching the elements of composition. All the students could see the composition being considered on the projector and the teacher had examples of good and poor use of grammar and construction.

A workshop was set up for the staff actually to produce teaching aids for the overhead projector, for the tape recorder, for the slide projector and for the flannel board. This workshop wasn't concerned with discussing the theory and extolling the virtues of the aids, but it centered on producing aids which would be used in each teacher's classes. Once the staff became secure in using the hardware, the ideas for their uses compounded. Their introduction in Lakeview learning groups became a reality.

An attempt was made by the administrators to use the aids in the faculty meetings to present group test score data, scheduling alterations and for other matters of general concern. No attempt was made to recommend a particular teaching aid. Instead, the teaching aids were considered an accepted part of the mode of operation. By example, it encouraged others to use the various teaching aids.

One member of the staff served as audio-visual aids coordinator. He concerned himself with equipment selection, training of students and teachers in equipment use and with the scheduling and upkeep of all the audio-visual apparatus. The materials used in the hardware, the slides, programs, films, recordings, charts, etc., were catalogued in the Instructional Materials Center.

Easy Access to Teaching Aids

The Instructional Materials Center was built in such a way that all of the teaching aids purchased and constructed could be kept in an orderly fashion for easy use by students and teachers.

Posters and charts purchased and constructed at Lakeview were stored in an area where they could be used easily. The work done in the field of biology with posters was particularly outstanding. The posters made one year were kept for use in succeeding years.

An extensive selection of maps was kept in the Instructional Materials Center, while others were checked out to various rooms. Both teachers and students could go to the map room and select what they needed from the collection amassed at the school. Access to all materials was open to both teachers and students. Encouragement was given to both to use them.

The transparencies made by the staff were considered to be school property and were to be filed in the Instructional Materials Center. This meant that people other than the originator could have the benefits of their use. It was agreed that if the board of education bought the supplies, then the finished product was the school's property and should be catalogued in the Instructional Materials Center. This sometimes was easier in theory than in practice. Teachers generally accepted this idea when the collection was built up large enough so a number of teachers could use it.

Materials Acquisition for Many Sources

Teaching aids came from many sources. Some were intricate and purchased at a high price from commercial companies; others were inexpensive and came for the asking. The auto mechanics teacher ordered some models of a car and engines. These were small models which could be taken apart and put back together.

Each part was labeled and its relationship to the whole was easy to see. When all the pieces were in their proper places, the motors would operate. Granted, this teaching aid was costly but it was very effective. The teacher who used it commented, "I've been teaching auto mechanics by verbal explanations and haven't been able to get through to all students for years. With the use of the model engine, I have universal understanding in the class now."

In business education the teachers wrote to insurance companies, investment houses and large wholesalers and got loads of materials for use in the business law and salesmanship classes. The teachers of the social studies tapped the federal government agencies for charts on social security, the organization of the executive branch of government and scores of other helpful materials. These aids were used with great advantage to the students in both class work and in independent study.

The armed forces had some discarded weather instruments which were used in the physical science classes. Lakeview students didn't learn of weather forecasting by reading, but they could actually visit the weather station on the grounds of the Lakeview School. Here again the purpose of building the weather station was to allow students to experience its operation. This was a demonstration of the theory that understanding should result from perceptual experience.

Teaching aids were of a variety of forms and were used in all content areas. Plastic sheets were turned into displays of voting machines for the social studies teachers. Radio kits were provided for industrial arts students to build their own sets. Racks of cloth were built for art students to see and touch various textile textures. Blank tapes were sent to foreign countries and they came back with recordings by the nations of the world. Over three hundred reproductions of paintings were added to the school's halls and classrooms to help students appreciate the art of the world.

The accumulation of teaching aids is a never-ending process. Once the staff saw the need and realized the advantage, the project was off the ground and the school was filled with teaching aids.

Teaching aids were not difficult to find when the staff was on the lookout for them. Students liked to collect and use them. From their pleasure at using them came increased understanding of the content under consideration.

Work Space and Materials Needed

At Lakeview certain areas were designated as project work stations. These were places where students and teachers could hammer, paste, type, develop film and make their learning aids. Too often school people expect activities of the noisy nature to go on outside of school. This, the staff felt, was not in keeping with the best learning practice. If noise was to be created in learning, then let the hammers pound and the noise level go up. So that these efforts wouldn't interfere with the quiet learning activities, zones in the building were set up for noisy activities and for the quiet activities.

A dark room was carved out of one end of a locker room. This was the place where photographic and transparency production or experimenting could take place. Another center was set up between the student study carrels and the teachers' offices for preparing teaching aids. Each of the laboratories for art, homemaking, science and industrial arts was set up for the production of teaching aids and for independent study as a part of the regular school day.

The school supplied as many materials as possible. These included art supplies, paper, tape, lumber, cloth, yarn, poster board, wax, etc. Moreover, all of the school's office machines were open for student use. Equipment was replaced at Lakeview more often from being worn out than from old age. What a pity it is when the converse is true in the schools!

The Important Factors

The important factor in considering the use of a particular teaching aid is not the hardware which makes it possible, but the ideas or material it presents. The question is not, "Shall we use an overhead projector?" The question is, "Will a transparency do the required job?" The same principle holds true for the recorders, flannel boards and all the other aids.

Some Lakeview teachers broke up film strips and used only one or two frames of a strip, for there was no justification in exposing students to superfluous material. One teacher used pieces of historical recordings as an apt introduction to presentations of twentieth century political thought. The entire recording was available for a student who wanted to hear it but for group instructional purposes, excerpts were enough. The important factor was to use what helped, regardless of where it was found and how much it was used.

The faculty agreed there was advantage in having students use the teaching aids in independent study. Thus, the storage was set up so they would be readily available to those who wanted to use them. Independent study time could be used with profit when the teaching aids were at hand for students to use.

One of the new specialists a school of the future will employ will be the teaching aid specialist who will support the teacher by preparing and finding multimedia instructional aids. We predict, as a result of the Lakeview experience, that schools will spend more money for technological aids. Students will use electronic tapes for drill work, view television tapes of significant idea presentations, listen to recordings and work through programmed learning materials to an extent not commonly envisioned. Both educators and policy makers for the schools must begin to close the gap between understanding of possible uses of aids and actual use of them.

Television Has a Place

Television has an undeniable place in the schools of the future. Quality content presentations, historical events and cases in point can be stored on video tape and presented to students at the appropriate time in the instructional process.

Unfortunately, too little use was made of television in the Decatur-Lakeview Plan. The numbers of places this important media would have fit into the plan are extremely high. For instance, a description in words or print of an "H" bomb explosion is a second-class experience for students compared to the actual viewing of the event on viedo tape.

In foreign language instruction, a close-up television shot of a French teacher pronouncing words, in which the teacher's mouth can be enlarged to the entire width of a screen, would, in aiding students, be far superior to a teacher's ability to show the mouth formation. In biology, typing and countless other subject areas, television has a place.

A teacher can go over a presentation by means of a video tape recording one, two, or a dozen times until it is absolutely correct. The equipment available today makes it as simple to record a video presentation as it is to make a voice tape.

Schools in the future will surely want to keep a library of television tape materials. Sometimes they will be used for large groups and at other times, they will be used by students in individual study.

Television has an undeniable place in the instructional process of our schools. The trick is to get our understanding of its use into the actual practice within the schools.

A closed circuit system was loaned to the Lakeview staff for trial and consideration for purchase. While it was strongly recommended by the staff for purchase because of the advantage it obviously held for instruction, it was vetoed for inclusion in the district budget. Television has a place in quality education, as even the limited experience at Lakeview showed.

Chapter
Eight

Programmed Learning

PROGRAMMED learning was another aid to the teacher's
instruction in the Decatur-Lakeview Plan. It is a worthwhile tool of instruction, but unfortunately it is used too
little to date in the schools generally. The number of programs
available for use from commercial publishers is increasing
at a rapid pace. At the same time many teachers are learning
program construction and introducing their own programs to
pupils.

Programmed instruction has great promise as an aid to
use before large group presentations and during independent
study time. Early research results indicate that programmed
instruction may profoundly modify many of our basic concepts of methodology of instruction. Even the less zealous
advocates maintain that a body of knowledge can be cov-

ered in approximately one-half the time with an increase of up to twenty-one per cent in achievement. This bold declaration is backed up by the application of the laws of learning we've known but not always used in day-to-day instruction.

Basically, all the mechanical boxes called "teaching machines" represent some variation of what is classically known as the tutorial or Socratic method of teaching. Each teaching machine, also, has some form of playback, whereby the student can compare his response to a question or problem with the correct response.

"Individualized instruction can become a reality by the use of programmed instruction," a Lakeview department report declared after a year's study of the subject.

The Learning Program Defined

Briefly described, the learning program is a logically related series of small steps through which the student will reason his way to subject-matter mastery. In the traditional method of presentation students are passive while being "told"; programmed instruction implies that the learners are active as they test their ideas and knowledge. Thus, the involvement students get in the learning process stimulates a desire for more positive learning.

Each step the learner takes with the teaching machine requires that he be attentive and that he be thinking. In addition, teaching machines or their learning programs offer the advantage of "errorless learning," as educational psychologists refer to the feature of teaching machines which immediately gives the student the correct answer for comparison to his response. Thus, the student is corrected before a misconception can develop. The teaching machine is a patient teacher, willing to answer every question at the learner's rate. The learning program pits the student against his own ability and does not put him in competition with his peers for attention of the tutor.

Lakeview teachers reported students had more questions about basic issues when they used programmed materials than when they read the same material in texts. An analysis of the questions indicated the reasons were positive. That is, the programmed instruction presentation caused depth thinking and clarified areas of question. Text study did neither.

The Use of Programmed Instruction Explained

Learning programs were most often housed in the Instructional Materials Center. Students could go to the Instructional Materials Center to get programs at their will and proceed through them at their own rate without the handicap of comparing one individual's rate with the rate of accomplishment of others.

At Lakeview, learning programs were used as supplements to group activity. In no case were programs used as the single instructional mode for whole courses. In almost all cases the programs were used as parts of courses with single content or process understanding objectives. For example, a program on the operation of the slide rule was used in mathematics and science classes, but the course itself was not taught wholly by learning programs. Programmed learning was an efficient way to teach this skill and, at the same time, save class time for more significant matters.

Some students with health problems who missed school used programmed instruction with profit. Although the staff felt these students did a good job in acquisition of content with the learning programs, the teachers felt their understanding would have been increased had they been doing the work with a class, as well as working with the learning programs. The point was made that discussion helps solidify knowledge acquired with programmed learning.

The staff used the programs whenever they could present ideas or skills in a way which would result in successful accomplishment. Some teachers effectively built their own learning programs for specific units of work. Youngsters worked on the programs outside of class, reserving the class time saved for discussion of material requiring further clarification and consideration. In a ninth grade English class, for example, a program was used on the parts of speech which saved a good chunk of class time for more depth study. The learning programs did the trick.

The Advantages of Programmed Learning Given

The shy individual, the non-communicative personality, and the unenthusiastic person all became full-time participants in the learning process when teaching machines were used. There was no reluctance in responding to a question by anyone since only the learner saw his response. Also, students got plenty of needed practice in manipulating and in rearranging facts.

One teacher found discussions of content easier with students who had been through a learning program than with those who had read the same material in a text. This was an English teacher who used a learning program for one group and a text for another in the study of verbals. She reported that instructional interaction was easier to generate on a higher level in the group with which she used the program. Youngsters liked to talk about the content when they were satisfied their mastery was complete.

The teaching machine allowed the student frequently to receive satisfaction from accomplishment. Instead of having a whole chapter to wade through before he got to exercises to see what he had learned, the happy learner found pleasure from seeing his progress as he learned. This satisfaction didn't get full realization when one had to wait for hours or days before relating a measure of knowledge with the full body of facts studied.

The program, itself, is the vital element in any teaching machine; the machine is only the external covering and has no instructional worth without an effective learning program. As a matter of fact, we found it expedient and helpful to give youngsters programs in file folders with cut-out slots for question and response, rather than building teaching machines. The hardware wasn't the critical element; it was the program that counted.

A consideration of the economics of construction of learning programs reveals it to be an enormously expensive operation as well. This might lead us to conclude that the development of learning programs, like other functions a local system cannot completely do for itself, might be the service of state departments of education or the United States Office of Education. On a small scale teachers can write some frames for use in specific application in their courses. Writing a learning program sharpens one's focus on the analysis of content. Even if the program isn't expert, the attempt will have some desirable advantage in analyzing content. Few Lakeview teachers who worked on program writing failed to agree to this.

Benefits of Staff Study Given

Programmed learning is based on Thorndike's law of effect, whereby an action which brings about a satisfactory result tends to be repeated. Another modified psychological learning principle employed is the Cartesian method of analyzing a problem into its smallest parts and proceeding from the simple to the complex. These, of course, are techniques of content analysis which capable instructors have always used.

At Lakeview it was found that faculty discussion of the theory of programmed learning had positive spill-over benefits in teacher content presentations. The principle of breaking knowledge into its logical parts and the principle of immediate reinforcement had application in teacher activity, as well as in learning program construction. It was interesting to note the frequency of use of programmed learning jargon in discussions not related to programmed learning. Once the Lakeview staff studied the psychology of programmed instruction, it permeated the faculty's thinking.

The Place of Programmed Instruction Given

The day will never come when the teaching machine will replace the teacher, but there is good reason to believe that it will not be long before programmed learning and teaching machines will be a central part of the instructional process in every course which is centered around the acquisition of fundamental objective facts. A teaching machine, like the printing press, is a mechanical aid for multiplying the effectiveness of instruction. Educators cannot afford to ignore it any more than they can afford to ignore the printing press.

The only task is to find programs which have application to

the school's content. Dedication to a belief in the merit of a learning program has little validity without the use of programs in day-to-day instruction. Some Lakeview teachers constructed their own programs, as mentioned earlier, though the consumption of many hours on a single frame didn't make volume production of learning programs possible. Those teachers who did write some unit programs gained a fuller understanding and appreciation of the theory of programming. More importantly, they demonstrated that educators in the field can write programs.

Since education is not only fact accumulation or assimilation, it is important to recognize the limits of teaching machines in instruction and to gear them to the behavior goals of the content being presented. After all, subject-matter mastery is only a means to the end of the school's instructional program. The teaching machine extends the teacher's skill as the X-ray machine broadens the physician's ability to perform his function. No X-ray machine has done anything but increase the doctor's skill. So too with teaching machines.

Learning programs must never be used as tests. One Lakeview staff member, a substitute teacher, had miserable results with a program when she used the program as a test. Were she not given help in understanding the theory of programming she would have lost the value of the program and perhaps done damage to the students' attitude about programmed instruction. Testing is intended to find right from wrong; programmed learning is intended to lead from a knowledge void to full understanding.

Employment of teaching machines with carefully structured programs allows the student to learn by doing and proceed at his own rate. The able student can romp through some phase of a course, while the slow learner can proceed at his own pace and still benefit. Thus individual differences are provided for and increased quality in education is approached.

Advantages of Learning Programs Isolated

Programmed learning through the use of teaching machines had these advantages at Lakeview in the areas where it was used:

1. Students progressed through content at their own rate.

2. Class time was not consumed with drill and routine questioning.

3. Class preparation by the teacher was tailored to the student level of accomplishment as structured by the learning program.

4. Content could be covered more rapidly; thus classes were devoted to concept development and its application.

5. The programs comprised an efficient diagnostic learning instrument.

6. Increased satisfaction from learning resulted for the students.

The most apparent worth of teaching machines and programmed learning was the emphasis placed on logical selection and presentation of ideas and facts in instruction. The teacher who investigated learning programs sharpened his skills in content presentation and, at the same time, came closer to recognizing individual differences by varying the rate and the amount of knowledge different students studied.

Uses of Programmed Instruction Mentioned

Programmed learning through teaching machines offered a clear and reliable route to increased quality in education.

Learning programs used in courses or in parts of courses at Lakeview included:

English	—Grammar, grades 7, 8 and 10; Poetry, grade 11
Foreign Language	—French, grades 9 and 10
Industrial Arts	—Electricity, grade 10
Mathematics	—Modern Mathematics, grades 7, 11 and 12; Equations, grade 9; Plane Geometry, grade 10
Music	—Theory of Music, grade 7
Science	—Energy, grade 8; Power, grade 8; Physics, grade 11; Chemistry, grade 12
Social Studies	—Flag and Illinois Constitution, grades 8 and 11; U.S. Constitution, grade 8

A few Lakeview teachers met once or twice a week to write programs for their own classes. The enterprise was profitable because of the understanding teachers gained of the theory of programming. The Lakeview experience demonstrated that few teachers will decry the use of programs once they appreciate the logic of their constructions.

Chapter
Nine

Student-Centered Activity:
Small Group Instruction

WITHOUT question, the most vital part of the Decatur-Lakeview Plan was the small group instruction. It was here that students reinforced and used knowledge learned in large groups and independent study; it was here that students formed attitudes; it was here that teachers made decisions which helped students assimilate content and develop the desire to increase skills and understandings.

A small group is the learning group in which the individual interacts with others. With some form of ability or achievement grouping in the organization, one can interact with others of the small group on his own level of understanding. An attempt must be made to establish a warm climate in which students are secure to ask, to propose, and to criticize. It is assumed that this kind of climate will bring about better learning, for when youngsters are in a warm, intimate psychological climate, they are free to make mistakes and profit from them.

The spotlight is on the student in the small group. In the traditional class of thirty pupils there can be little real discussion. In a fifty-five minute period each student has only a small portion of time to express or to test his ideas. If one student does claim a large segment of the class time with his problem, it is at the expense of the other class members. Recitation is somehow more appropriate to the traditional size class, while discussion becomes practical in a group of seven to fifteen students. In a traditional class there is a tendency for the teacher to talk too much, at the expense of the learners. At Lakeview the large group sessions were for teacher presentations and the small groups belonged to the students.

The small group teacher can give students more individual attention, even ignoring the other instructional advantages possible in the small groups. Whether or not this opportunity is utilized depends upon the orientation and skill of the instructor. The small group does offer more opportunity for the student to ask questions and to test his ideas than does a class of thirty. Size alone makes a difference.

One of the really new requirements of teachers in the Decatur-Lakeview Plan was the work teachers were expected to do with students in a one-to-one or small group situation. Before student behavior in a new learning situation will change, teachers need to operate in a new and different manner. The role of the teacher in a small group class is paramount in setting the guidelines and forming the operating pattern of the Plan.

Small group activities are characterized by a high degree of student participation. The teacher becomes the advisor, the resource person and the tutor for group members.

The barriers of communication created by row on row of desks are torn down when a small group of students arrange chairs in a circle or sit around a table. At Lakeview it was found helpful to remove the teacher's desk from the seminar rooms, thereby requiring the teacher to sit around the table or in an armchair in a circle with the class. The effective teacher refrains from giving again the lecture already presented in the large group and becomes concerned with serving as content counselor and materials resource guide when

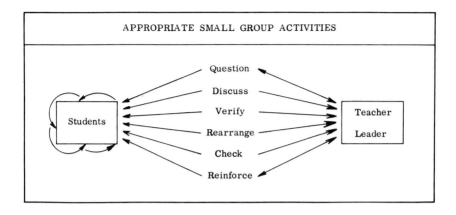

needed. It takes a highly competent teacher to know when to ask the critical question, when to suggest the needed source of further information, and when to use a restatement of a proposition as the basis for increased understanding. The real role of the teacher is at its highest when instructor and learner work in the small group on an academic consideration.

Finding the Way Toward Small Group Instruction

In the planning stage of the Decatur-Lakeview Plan, it was assumed that small group instruction would be an easy and automatic role for the staff. Such did not prove to be the case. Teachers found it difficult to cast themselves in the role of listener, of advisor, of group participant. Some staff members found it difficult to make on-the-spot judgments as to when professional assistance in group activity was appropriate, even necessary, and when it wasn't. The most effective small group teachers are those who listen to a student discussion and know when to straighten out ideas or to suggest different approaches to problem situations.

The administrative selection at Lakeview of one area, the social studies, as a model for total staff consideration in the in-service training program for small group teacher behavior, got other areas off the track in setting up procedures for small group work. The operational procedures and techniques used in social studies were not fully appropriate for all other content areas, particularly English and science. Discussion is easier to stimulate in social studies than in the grammar phase of English, for example. The Lakeview staff soon concluded that care should be taken to develop a model for small group instruction in each of the content areas within a school in the in-service program.

The Lakeview department heads were charged with the responsibility for developing a model of small group techniques suited to their content area. They did it ably. Each department area set down the kinds of things teachers in the small groups could do in their area. Some subjects implied the use of work sheets to give a direction to the group. Others did not. All the small groups, though, were organized around student interaction and characterized by a high level of involvement on the part of the learner. The teacher's task was to keep the group on the beam and to avoid irrelevant discussion.

Characteristics of Small Group Classes

Education is a feeling for facts as well as a knowledge of them. Therefore, an attempt was made to treat attitudes and feelings about content in the small group. Such understandings come from student involvement on the learner's level of reference. It is through the interaction of the small group that students should develop appreciations and understandings. Even a casual observer at Lakeview noticed the increased consideration of meanings and implications in these small group sessions. Facts became a vehicle for thinking and not an end in themselves.

How often have we heard teachers say, "I didn't really understand my subject until I taught it?" This situation results from the teachers' use of facts in developing concepts. In college, teachers heard about their subject, in teaching they used it. Small group participation can have the same result for students if it is so structured.

Discussion in small groups was based on teacher-managed objectives. While students set up the problems for consideration they were necessarily in concert with course goals. The depth and breadth of small group activity must be the continuous concern of the teacher. This accounts for the need for alertness to day-to-day, even minute-to-minute, class progress by the teacher in each small group.

No two small groups are ever the same, and exact preplanned minute preparation is unrealistic. The objective of individualizing instruction is lost if an attempt is made to keep all the small groups together. Student accomplishment, as demonstrated by the small group class activities, is measured only against a standard of the group members' abilities.

The small group was the source of countless self-assumed and, sometimes, teacher-encouraged or assigned projects and activities. It was most difficult to stimulate real independent study. Teacher suggestion of written references and of resource people helped satisfy the need for getting started on an investigation project. The more effective the small group the more diversity existed in the small group activities. The goal of individualizing instruction became a reality as a result of small group experiences.

A visit to a Lakeview small group in algebra might find discussion occupying almost all the class time. Here students discuss the "unknowns" of mathematics in their language, challenge each other and establish relationships with concepts previously studied. The teacher enters and withdraws as the pace of progress requires. It is never assumed that discussion alone is the goal of a small group. Students profit from listening to their peers, from doing mathematics problems, for instance, and checking them with the teacher or other students. Some recitation is necessary to accompany almost any sound discussion. This is particularly true in courses where attitude development is less important than process understanding.

Planning for Small Group Instruction

To begin small group instruction without careful explanation of objectives and procedures is to doom such instruction to failure. Students who find themselves in a small group for the first time without some orientation cannot operate in any way differently than in their traditional size classes. They are so used to being told to give short answers on teacher-determined cues that students are at first insecure with the free exploration of ideas. It is necessary to have a school-wide understanding, as well as a departmental emphasis, on the place of the small group in the total program. This was achieved by an all-school assembly, by articles in the school newspaper and by the teachers' efforts to explain their specific goals. The problem of learning how to learn in this type of school organization must not be overlooked in the inauguration of such a program.

It isn't enough to make a declaration about desiring student involvement in the small groups. It takes patience and time on the teacher's part to develop the knack for drawing students into group work. If an instructor of a small group doesn't get an immediate reaction from a group, he can't retreat into a verbal haven; but he must ask again and again those questions that ignite a flame of interest for the students.

Getting the Group "Going"

Some staff members find it effective to appoint or have the small group elect a student leader. This leader is charged with the responsibility for regulating the pace, compensating for lags in progress and involving all the group members. This tends to take authority away from the teacher and, at the same time, affords good opportunities for student leadership development. The teacher has more chance for understanding what students know as he becomes the group observer. More than once the passive, diffident student benefited when he was selected group leader.

Some small group teachers divided their group of fifteen or more students into two groups with real benefit. A United States history teacher found this to be a way to increase the involvement of students. This teacher sat between the two groups and entered whichever group needed his help.

A sophomore English teacher reported that students seemed to do a better job of preparation for student-centered small group classes than for the traditional size class. He maintained that students didn't like being unprepared when other classmates would do the questioning. Somehow adolescents of this age are more concerned with the opinions of their peers than with the attitude of the teacher. This is not to say that the small group organization will result in full preparation on the part of every student, but it is to say that there was more preparation in the small group organization than there had been in the traditional class.

A science teacher used a class observer with profit. Each day one student was selected as the observer. He was to keep track of the amount of participation, serve as a summarizer at the end of the session and evaluate the group's progress. This helped the observer in his future group participation, and served as a review of the day's activity for all the class.

After the first year the staff felt that a major weakness of the small group operation was a lack of active participation on the part of some students. A heated controversy developed on this question and hasn't been resolved yet. Some thought it unrealistic to assume that all students would be active in every small group activity. The general feeling was that the human machine isn't filled with limitless energy and that some passive observance is worthwhile and desired. The point is this: The small group structure doesn't guarantee that everyone will be highly involved in group work, but it does provide the opportunity for more students to participate more often than in a traditional class of thirty. Small group classes increase the opportunity for learning, but they don't necessarily insure it.

Helping Students in Small Groups

Selection of student leaders for the small groups was particularly critical at the beginning of each school year. There have been two approaches used, each having succeeded in some content areas and with some teachers and each having met with some failure. The first method was having students select their own leaders. The motive here was to give a leadership role to the student whom other students would follow. The belief was that students would be more active in course work when the person with the greatest favor was moderator. On the other hand, other staff members felt that the primary qualities in the leader should be knowledge and initiative rather than popularity alone.

Of course, the ideal was a highly accepted student well grounded in content, well motivated, and skillful in involving others in the group work. An adolescent with such skill is not often found. Therefore, too much should not be expected of the student leaders until they have had teacher assistance and experience.

One teacher had a series of sessions with his student leaders to discuss purposes and to give suggestions on leadership behavior. Included in the questions these student leaders discussed were: "When do you ask non-verbal students questions? What do you do if no one in the group understands a concept or doesn't have a fact at hand? How do you shift the spotlight from the student who takes too much of the group's attention? What is important to consider in a class? What is unimportant? How active should the leader be in a group activity?"

An instructor of a small group in biology constructed a sociogram to determine the composition of sub-groups in the small group. He reported that this was beneficial and became a strong advocate of establishing leadership by this means. He felt this was better than voting for a leader or appointing one. As in so many phases of instruction, it is not wise to suggest only one method of leadership selection. More research and study needs to be done on this topic.

The leadership role was often passed around from student to student. As the group gained familiarity and cohesiveness, the leadership role became less vital, we think, and the group accepted informal leadership and became responsive to it.

There is real advantage in rotating the role, for leadership qualities are developed, they are not inherited. Therefore, emphasis was placed on giving all students as much leadership opportunity as possible at Lakeview.

One of the important purposes of small group activity was to strengthen basic skills of speaking, reading, writing and listening. Some instructors found merit in giving students new material in class and then asking them to interpret it in the same class. Often this interpretation was written by the students and then the teacher evaluated it immediately so that the students could compare opinions.

Strengthening Small Group Instruction

The kernel of strength in any small group instruction is the role the teacher can play in helping individualize instruction. When a teacher finds a weakness in the student, professional attention can be given to strengthen this weakness or help the student compensate for it.

A business education teacher learned that a student in basic business (9th grade introductory course) failed tests, but was an able participant in the class discussions. The teacher gave the next test orally and found the results were amazing in terms of positive knowledge of content. This boy blocked on tests owing to a reading inability and an emotional resistance to tests built up over years of failing tests. The instructor gave a series of tests orally and then, after a number of successful experiences, asked the student to do a part in writing and a part orally. Gradually the teachers increased the parts of the tests taken in writing and decreased the oral testing. Noticeable improvement was demonstrated in the student's ability to profit from tests; the student's reading deficiency wasn't overcome, but his emotional block to testing was reduced. What teacher in a traditional group has the opportunity to understand the students so well.

Small group instruction becomes a stronger force in the student's educational life when it is successful for him. Each day every student should be given some sense of pride in accomplishment. The teacher has to dodge in and out of the class progress to make this aim a reality. The small group instruction was strengthened after adequate time elapsed between the Teacher-Leader's understanding of the operational objectives of the small groups and his communication of this to the class through behavior. That is, the Teacher-Leader had to demonstrate that students could freely express their doubts about ideas and ignorance of facts without reproach by the teacher or fear of a low grade.

Time was the greatest aid in improving the student involvement in small groups. Students coming from teacher-centered elementary and secondary school experiences did not find it a part of their pattern of class behavior to ask basic questions or to display dismay at what they didn't know. With experience in the small groups this changed and students became less defensive and more objective about what they did and didn't know.

Individualizing instruction is easier said than done. It requires the concentration of the teacher on the varying abilities and interests of each student. The guidance counselors were helpful in sharing with the instructors of the small groups their knowledge and understanding of students. Such information can only serve as a clue to giving the teacher background data to help make the needed on-the-spot decisions in class. The real test of what a student requires in terms of scholastic assistance comes in his performance with subject matter in the small group.

Varying Instructional Needs of Learners

The administrator should constantly remind the staff about varying instructional needs of students. Staff meetings, bulletins, team meetings and individual informal conferences are the administrator's means to this end.

The project plan of studying a unit of work helps in the humanities and in the practical arts in this regard. When students select their own area of concentration, whether it is a study of foods or consumer buying in homemaking or the theory of freedom or early warfare in social studies, there is a real opportunity for the teacher to make suggestions to the student that help him understand the content and develop ability and skill in areas of weakness. A boy who is highly interested in automobiles will accept grammatical instruction more easily when he is working on an individual research paper on the history of automobiles, rather than through the traditional English grammar workbook. A girl who is deeply concerned about future marital possibilities will do a better job of composition when the rules of rhetoric are applied in a theme on a subject of her interest.

Most small groups at Lakeview began with a discussion evaluating the lectures. This served as a clue to what had been assimilated and what needed further study. It was from listening to the small group evaluations of the lectures that the Teacher-Leader could form a base for deciding with the Teacher-Presenter what needed to be presented in the next large group meeting. During the teaching team meetings these matters were discussed.

In the Decatur-Lakeview Plan almost fifty per cent of a student's day was filled with small group participation as contrasted with thirty per cent in independent study and twenty per cent in large group presentations. This distribution of time indicated the importance the staff placed on small group activity. As time goes on and the program develops we would hope that the independent study time would increase and the small group instructional time decrease.

There had to be an objective in the Teacher-Leader's mind for each small group meeting. This objective was subject to change once the class began, of course, but a discussion group's instructional worth diminished if the Teacher-Leader had no objective for each meeting.

Some teachers were concerned with communications within a group and kept participation charts. Two crude studies indicated a low correlation between rate of individual participation and content understanding as measured by course tests. There was a high correlation noted between the mean scores in a group with a high amount of participation and a low amount of participation in the small group and test scores. The implication seems clear that the frequency of participation helped all the group assimilate ideas, but not necessarily the group's most articulate participants. This is another fertile area of educational research the program has uncovered.

Determining Specifications for Learning Groups

Most Lakeview small groups were set up by some grouping specifications. While the most common means of grouping was on the basis of standardized test scores, other unusual specifications for grouping were set up. In a science class all pre-engineering students were in one group. Thus, intended vocational choice was the specification. In a social studies class the group specification was the verbal frequency of the student; all the quiet, less verbal students were in one group and all the verbal, active discussants were in another. There has been a suggestion for further, and quite promising, specifications on the basis of age, sex, and other behavior and interest patterns.

Once one narrows the span of achievement in a small group, the scope of activities becomes helpfully restrictive. We welcomed this because it allowed groups to operate on a common base in an area of related interest and need. This made it more difficult, however, for the teacher to gear the content to the students' level in some groups, particularly in groups of slow learners. The difficulty of the task made the success, once it was achieved, all the sweeter. In a heterogeneous group the able learners carried the group work on their level, often ignoring the lack of understanding of the slow student. In the grouped class the goal became more nearly suited to each member. As in all types of organization for instruction, there was frequently greater teacher effort and concern given to the slow learners' group. The grouping employed at Lakeview sharpened the problem for these students who might have gone without identification or have been ignored in a heterogeneous group. The diversity of student activities was great, even in the grouped sections. This was, of course, in harmony with the program's objectives.

SMALL GROUP COMPOSITION POSSIBILITIES		
Method	Advantages	Possible Content Areas
Achievement Groups	Relatively common content range may result in more rapid learning for group members.	Mathematics Foreign Language Music
Vocational Choice Groups	Common interests may result in possibility for appropriate instruction emphasis.	Science Industrial Arts
Verbal Facility Groups	Similar verbal inclinations may result in warmer group communication.	Social Studies
Sex Determined Groups	Maturation and interest compatibility may result in group cohesiveness.	Art Science English
Emotional Maturity Groups	Personality characteristic matching may result in good group rapport.	Homemaking Social Studies
Friendship Groups	Security and familiarity may result in increased participation in class work.	Business Education

SMALL GROUP COMPOSITION POSSIBILITIES (continued)		
Method	Advantages	Possible Content Areas
Poor School Attendance Groups	Support and common problems may result in increased understanding.	English Social Studies
Reading Level Groups	Reading ability similarities may result in more self-understanding and added personal security.	English Science Social Studies

Each team determined the specification for the small groups in their content area. The guidance staff supplied the data, got the recommendations from other staff members on the students' instructional needs and identified students for appropriate small groups. It then fell to the assistant principals to program the students.

The purpose of setting up specifications for the small groups was to attempt to bring together those students who could establish some solidarity within the group. The assumption was that students could be supporting in a beneficial way when the group of which they were members could develop some cohesiveness.

Students moved in and out of the small groups as teachers saw fit. This was easier to do in a small-large group schedule than in a traditional schedule because of the many more groups meeting.

In a traditional schedule if there are two hundred students in a freshman class, there are usually six or seven English classes, for example. In the Lakeview schedule there were seventeen possible groups for any student to be in. The increased number of groups to schedule opened greater possibilities of movement, but this did complicate the scheduling process.

Quintilian, a Roman teacher of almost two thousand years ago, had something to say worthwhile to us today. Quintilian's advice was:

Do not neglect the individual student. He should be questioned and praised . . . he should strive for victory, yes, but it must be arranged so that he gains it. In this way, let us draw forth his powers with both praise and rewards.

It is significant to note that Quintilian's advice is in precise agreement with the modern learning theory. Researchers point out that youngsters learn best when they can achieve success in performing learning activities. Students need as much individual instruction as teachers can give. A worthy operational teaching aim of the Decatur-Lakeview Plan was to structure class work so that each student would realize a sense of accomplishment as frequently as possible. The small groups helped make this possible.

Generalizing About Small Groups

We can generalize by saying that the small groups which were the most productive of student involvement were those led by teachers fresh from their university preparation. The reason is that there was less for the beginning teacher to learn about instructional behavior. On the other hand, this generalization was discredited by several examples of experienced teachers who did a splendid job of creating student-centered small groups at Lakeview. This did not come without a great deal of painstaking work, however, on the part of the experienced staff.

The small groups offered the greatest challenge to the teacher, for here contact with the student was intimate. Here teachers could observe students while working, discussing, and reciting. The great task of motivating students to want to learn became individualized in the small group. It was through the active cooperation of the learner in carry-out instructional procedures that the purposes of the small group were best fulfilled.

It has been generally concluded that students will do about what they are expected to do and be about what they are expected to be, within the limits of their ability. Those teachers who expected students to accept responsibility for thinking, for reorganizing thoughts, and for being active group participants were usually rewarded with such student behavior. On the other hand, those instructors who had opposite expectations were likewise able to expect comparable student performance in the small groups. The key to the value of the small groups was, more often than not, the Teacher-Leader and his ability to bring out student reactions and expressions.

The Lakeview experience, verified by discussions with educators from other small-large group schools, indicated that the small group phase of the program was the most difficult to operate and the most worrisome to the staff.

It is, indeed, unfortunate that so many teachers subscribe to the belief that there is no pain so great as the one suffered from the un-delivered lecture! The real pay-dirt of instruction comes from the associations that students and teachers have in a give-and-take dis-cussion. Often lectures, and discussion in small groups, do more for the one transmitting than the one receiving. The small group is the station at which every youngster gets his opportunity for expression and self-development.

Chapter
Ten

Teacher-Centered Activity: Large Group Instruction

L ARGE group instruction, when given in a carefully planned manner, can be a critical element in successful instruction. It should be stressed, however, that the nature and purpose of the large group instruction demands that it be combined with small group activity and individual or independent study. Large group and small group instruction are like love and marriage: you shouldn't have one without the other!

The nature of the learning activity determines the group size in which each activity is appropriate and, of course, the converse is true. In large groups content and background information which builds on the learner's previous experience is given. This is done by stimulating lectures, by the systematic use of films, film strips, recordings and the overhead projector. In addition, it is appropriate to test, to give

114

basic assignments, and to employ resource specialists. Listening, seeing and supervised individual activities are appropriate for the large
group.

It saves time and talent to perform these activities daily for one
or two hundred students, rather than repeat them five or more times
for traditional size groups. Schools providing for large group instruction often find beneficial the increased use of resource experts: doctors,
the industrial chemists, the artists or skilled craftsmen. The Lakeview experience has shown that these valuable resource people don't
mind, and even like to talk to the large groups.

We would argue that a student can take a test in a group of two
hundred with as much advantage as in a group of thirty, twenty or
ten. The same reasoning is involved in lecture presentations. This
aspect of instruction is a quasi-passive operation for the learner. He
can get the facts which build concepts in content explanations in the
large group as well as in a small group.

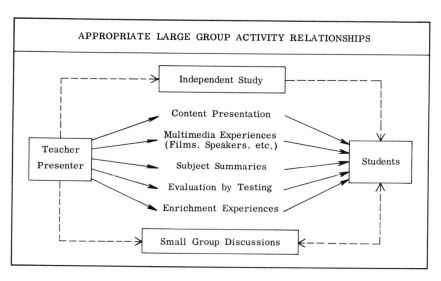

Teachers tended to be better at lecturing, the Lakeview experience
showed, when they had the added time for preparation which a small-
large group schedule buys. Also, many teachers were stimulated by a
large number of students in the lecture hall. Staff members went to
painstaking effort to prepare a crisp lecture supported by helpful
visual aids for a large group.

Experience has clearly demonstrated that large group instruction can be as helpful in grades seven and eight as in grades eleven and twelve. The key to success of large group instruction was to gear the content and work to the learner's level of understanding.

Adequate Preparation Should Precede Large Group Instruction

Before any large group instruction is attempted, the wise administrator and teacher will introduce students to the purpose and the suggested procedures to be used in the large group. Such matters include seat assignment, materials needed for note-taking, procedures for leaving the lecture hall, etc. The ground rules should be established by the staff and communicated to the students at the beginning of any program of large group instruction.

Large group instruction is easy to introduce. As teachers, we know more about it than about small group work, because this is how we were taught, and most of our students have been acclimated to the large group by eight to twelve years of previous school experience. It is a serious error, though, to confuse ease of implementation with excellence of operation. Quality large group classes require careful planning.

There must be an intensive in-service education program before inauguration of large group instruction. This is where someone must exert the leadership role, for the curriculum changes only as teachers change. Therefore, any program for increased quality needs to begin with the staff and should be a continuous process of development, evaluation and refinement. As the Talmud says, "We are never able to see our work completed, nor are we permitted to cease in our efforts."

Too often we hear of concern about student discipline in a large group. This is a straw man. Adolescents at Lakeview responded favorably to well-prepared and well-presented lectures. Also, peer group pressures caused high school students not to "want to be different" by misbehavior in the large groups. Concern over discipline was more appropriate in the small groups where youngsters were active in their self-expression!

Five Decisions Concerning the Large Group

There are five decisions in each school that need to be universally accepted in the organization of large group instruction. An administrator who wishes to see a successful large group program will do well to involve the staff in these decisions or, at least, get their general support.

First, what will the purpose of the large group be . . . basal content preparation or for enrichment? In Pelham, New York, the staff would argue that the large group is to be used almost exclusively for enrichment experiences; for basic concepts are expected to be understood before the large group session.

At Lakeview, we advocated the use of large groups for the presentation of fundamental ideas or fact. The stated purpose of the large group will determine what goes on in the small groups and, to a lesser extent, in independent study. That is, the cycle of content presentation, individual study and discussion reinforcement must begin somewhere. Perhaps some student groups don't need the motivation the Lakeview staff felt the large groups gave for content comprehension.

Second, a decision needs to be made about the student composition of the group. That is, is this to be for all students on a grade level, irrespective of ability or interest in the specific content area? This decision varies among the schools using varying class size. Experiences in at least two schools indicate, however, that low ability students (especially in reading skill) profit a great deal from large groups. These students responded to quality lectures and got more from verbal and visual communication than from written communication.

Third, responsibility for this instruction must be decided upon. Some schools, unfortunately, rotate the large group responsibility among members of the teaching team. We regard this as a disadvantage because some teachers don't have the ability for good large group instruction; therefore, mediocrity is spread on a larger horizon. It takes time to become skillful at working with large groups and the greater the skill of the staff in this activity, the more beneficial the activity.

Fourth, there is need to do some serious thinking about the number and length of large group meetings in each area. That is, how often and for how long should large groups meet? For example, a skill course, like industrial arts, may require the use of fewer large groups than, perhaps, world history. Skill development courses generally have less need for sessions of explanation than for periods of practice. The number of large groups per week or per month will vary according to content and grade level if the number is based on the individual course and specific students' needs.

It seemed wise at Lakeview to begin with fewer large groups than seemed ideal. Enrollment per group and frequency of meetings were increased as students and teachers became accustomed to them. This, unfortunately, is sometimes the opposite approach used by innovators who have unsuccessful large group programs.

Students don't learn from listening, but from wanting to listen. Ideally, the large group meetings are anxiously anticipated by the learner. But it takes a lot of teacher planning to make this a reality. Large group planning must keep the supporting roles of independent study and small group instruction in perspective. Large group activities should be the starting point for independent study.

The length of the large group meetings demands careful consideration. Research on the attention span of learners is mounting. It is a fact that instructional effectiveness diminishes as the length of a presentation session increases. The Lakeview population responded best to the shorter lecture period of about thirty minutes. Teachers found that with practice their presentations could be adequately given in twenty-seven minutes.

If it is true that the attention span is taxed after a half-hour, then lectures must be shortened. Teachers can condense lectures into half-hour sessions, though this takes time, experience and self-discipline. There is no reason why the number of sessions can't be increased if more time is needed. For example, maybe chemistry demands a daily half-hour lecture, while algebra can be presented in three weekly lectures. The point is made best by the old proverb: "The mind can grasp no more than the seat can endure."

Testing can be as meaningful in a half-hour as in an hour. Try it and see! Tests which uncover student understanding or lack of it do not need to have the point made by item repetitions. A test can serve both its evaluative and, we should hope, teaching functions by its quality construction, not by its detail or length.

Fifth, the final important issue that needs to be resolved is the coordination of the large group activities with small group activities and independent study. One can begin by constructing an anatomy of learning for the school. Once one has identified the form, the structure of large and small groups, he can begin with making decisions about the substance of the instructional process. Will the team be formally organized with a chairman or master or head teacher? Will the content be pre-determined or constructed from week to week?

Techniques for Large Group Instruction

Large group teachers used various techniques in instruction. These we mention as the most widely used.

Often the interrogative statement was made with a pause before the teacher gave the answer in the large group. Instead of declarative statement upon declarative statement, interrogative sentences caught the students' attention. This varied the pace and invited the ever-wandering mind to return to the designated path.

The overhead was the basic tool for large group instruction. The color overlays were appealing to learners. The turning on and off of the machine was another call for mental attention.

Work sheets with missing facts or with unanswered questions were sometimes used effectively in large group presentations. These helped students relate as well as remember facts.

In the large groups it is recommended that appeal be made to the visual as well as to the auditory sense. Once a teacher concentrated on developing visuals many possibilities arose in all content areas. Since we had not been introduced to them as students, we sometimes overlooked their possibilities as teachers. We found that some teachers just could not develop visual presentations of ideas even though they could verbalize well. In the team meetings visual presentation was discussed. Both the large group and small group teachers worked on the presentation of transparencies.

The large groups were intended to be teacher-centered. Therefore, the pace varied as the Teacher-Presenter sensed the mood of the group. In the large group the Teacher-Leader was ever on the alert for ways to interest students in following the Teacher-Presenter's lesson.

Television offers a tremendous potential in large group instruction. Teachers can do on television video recordings the things they can't do in front of a group—bring the President's own words into the class, show the race riots in Mississippi, or enlarge a cell to the full size of a television screen.

Imagination in Facility Use Is Sometimes Needed

Before a building remodeling and addition program was begun, the Decatur-Lakeview Plan went on in a traditional-type building. The cafeteria was used as the large group room. When the addition was added to take care of increasing enrollments, it was decided to build two large group rooms specifically for this type of instruction. The point is this: Lakeview demonstrated that a large group program could be inaugurated in a traditional-type building, even though specially designed facilities are more functional.

Facilities are more often an excuse for than a real barrier to beginning large group instruction. Most buildings have a cafeteria, a study hall (the old ones particularly) or some other area that can be converted for lecture use. There is little sacred about a wall. Overcoming an unreasonable reverence for the antiquity of a wall can result in exciting new possibilities for instruction. More consideration should be given to altering existing school structures in American schools to facilitate better ways of teaching.

Recording Lectures Serves Students and Teachers

At Lakeview it was valuable to record some of the lectures on a portable recorder-amplifier used by the Teacher-Presenter. This concurrent operation, recording and amplifying, made operation simple. The tapes had two real advantages. For teachers they were a valuable in-service tool. When a teacher heard his lecture repeated, it was amazing what adjustments were made in lecturing technique. The tape was even better than team members in suggesting to the Teacher-Presenter that he was talking too slowly or too fast, and the former seemed to be the more frequent correction. For students who were absent or wanted to go over the lecture again, this was of invaluable assistance. The lecture tapes should be stored in the Instructional Materials Center, easily available for student use.

Reasons for Large Group Instruction

The motive for large group instruction is important. As far as we know, no one who has systematically and effectively used large group instruction has saved money on staff. While there is economy in student time in assembling in a large group, more preparation time should be given for the staff preparation. Thus, the staff time saved is redeployed to preparation time. The economy in staff comes in using the person most frequently for the thing he does best. In addition, more funds are required for equipment and supplies for the large groups. The only defensible motive for large group instruction is that it makes increased learning possibilities available for students.

It is unfortunate that the name for these groups is "large group instruction," for this emphasizes the abundance of students and not the activities which go on in this group.

In summary, then, the functions of the large group at Lakeview were:

1. To establish the relevancy and background of the lesson.

2. To provide background concepts and to trigger recall to previous experience.

3. To stimulate inquiry.

4. To focus on important detail and to isolate basal ideas.

5. To provide enrichment information or to correlate related knowledge.

6. To pull together a summary of ideas or process presented.

7. To utilize the talent for presenting ideas among faculty as fully as possible.

8. To employ outside resource people effectively.

Quality Group Instruction Doesn't Just Happen

Better large group instruction results from informal conferences over coffee and formal meetings with the staff, once there is a real dedication to use of large groups. Conferences with other large group teachers and visits to other schools have some value; journals stimulate thinking; consultants sharpen the focus on the specific content situations. But the real worth results when the teachers who employ it do the thinking, the talking, the planning, and then the acting.

The kernel of large group instruction was not in listening to a multitude of words, but in having organized experiences increase understanding and motivate the learner to want to know, to seek, to do.

We would advocate the principle of gradualism in implementing large group instruction or in any kind, for that matter, of change in instructional organization. A schedule was developed at Lakeview whereby some large group instruction was begun on each grade level, seven through twelve, but all courses did not meet in the large groups during the first year of the Plan's operation. An attempt was made to have one course in each grade level in the large group pattern during this first year. Thus, all teachers of a content area could view the large group in preparation for its full use during the second year of the Plan's operation.

It was interesting to note the satisfaction and favor with which all grade levels received the large group lectures during the first year, although all individual students did not rate the large groups as better than the traditional class.

Students found they could operate successfully in the one or two courses they took in small and large groups, and at the same time were able to use the traditional class of twenty-five as a yardstick for judgment. This gradual reorganization caused not one adverse student or parent reaction when the small and large groups were fully operative in the second and third years of the Plan's operation.

Chapter
Eleven

Knowledge Acquisition
and Learning Reinforcement:
Independent Study

T HE third prong of the Decatur-Lakeview Plan was independent study. It was vital to the success of the large and small groups. Independent study was, of course, a student-centered activity; but it demanded constant stimulation by the teacher of the small group and the presenter of the large group.

Study, broadly defined, is the investigation of a problem. Study is an active individual process (even when shared) which is highly personal in its effect. The goal of the large group instruction was to present ideas in such a way that students would want to learn more by personal study. The aim of the small group discussion was to give students an outlet for what they learned in their independent study.

Student-Assumed and Teacher-Assigned Study

Independent study was distinguished from guided study in that it was done without the direct supervision of a teacher. The teacher was concerned with its motivation and evaluation, however. There were two broad levels of independent study, teacher-assigned and student-assumed. The former was often called "homework" or was any outside-of-class assignment. Both students and teachers had no problem understanding what this was supposed to be. The challenge came in getting students to *want* to do it. Study assumed by the student was the higher level of independent study. It took place as a result of a learner's desire to seek more knowledge or skill and was measured by its breadth and depth. Here again the measure must be the student's ability and personal mental characteristics.

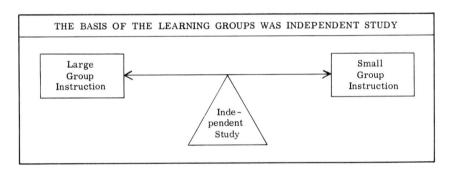

A student with an interest in a topic, art of the nineteenth century for example, may seek all the information he can on the subject of the art of this period, on the lives and background of the artists, on the media used and so forth. This was apt to be an outgrowth of a history class, the result of a literary study or the particular focus of a general art course. Teachers who wanted their students to pursue this kind of work encouraged it by giving small group time for students to explain and discuss their studies. Once again, the emphasis was on the individual attention given the student.

Teacher-directed study is determined by the student's understanding of a particular subject. Student-assumed study, on the other hand, was the expression of a particular interest by an individual student. Both levels could not be expected of all students from every teacher. In some areas students wanted to do more independent study than in others.

Quality of Independent Study Variation

The quality of both kinds of study varied greatly. Quality was bounded by the learner's ability, his motivation and his responsiveness, and the worth of the activity to him. A very slow learner with limited capacity was capable of both kinds of study. More than likely it would be uncomplicated and narrow, yet it was good for this student in view of his ability. The rate of accomplishment was often slow for the student of low ability. To demand the same level of independent study from all students was to defeat the fundamental goal of individual development.

On the other hand, the able and ambitious student performed both kinds of independent study with speed and facility. Teachers had to know the capacity of their student to measure its real value. Before a teacher could make a helpful suggestion to a student, he had to know the student's capabilities and interests.

As has been said, it was a serious error to assume that only the able learner could perform independent study with profit, for the measure of worth of independent study is the individual student's potential. The independent effort of one student wasn't ever to be judged against that of another student, but against his own inherent potential.

Motivation and Direction in Independent Study

It was unrealistic to think that all study would or should be student-assumed. Adolescents need both inspiration and direction. First, students need to have background information for almost any important topic. If teachers can't give students all the facts, they can suggest resource materials and sources of information. Second, an adolescent's interests, diverse as they may be, have limits. These limits can be stretched as a result of quality instruction. Even greater than the restriction of interest is the barrier of time. It is folly to believe that a high school student should go into every subject in breadth and depth. Here we see the need to know the student and his interests, both personal and scholastic. A student interested in automobiles can find interesting possibilities for study of this topic in mathematics, in calculating speed; in English and history, in reading novels and in studying the historical background of transportation; in art, in studying automotive design; and in science, in learning about the operation of engines. Effective teachers prescribed study activity based on general understanding needs and sought to motivate students to pursue study in the personal area of interest if applicable to the subject being taught.

Self-assumed study, except in a few cases, did not occur without teacher encouragement. The importance of the teacher cannot be underscored enough in all phases of the independent study operation. Problem-solving methods were taught by staff so students could pursue their interest in a given topic. Methods of problem solving were basic, but they were not enough. The small group teacher had to remain forever sensitive to possible cues of independent study interest.

Calculated Effort for Independent Study

Teachers who stimulated student-assumed study had to make a strong effort to get the job done. There were four principles to keep in mind in this regard. It required that the staff be willing to spend countless hours with individual students. Independent study motivation requires individual instruction of each student. Second, teachers needed to define the diverse methods of possible investigations. The teacher's job is to teach processes and procedures which the learners can apply to topics of investigation. Third, teachers had to know the students' personalities to be able to make use of individual interests. The relationship teachers have with students working independently is a highly personal and, it is hoped, an informal one. Fourth, students needed encouragement and recognition as they performed an independent study assignment. A single letter grade or a brief written comment isn't enough recognition.

When a student in a small group completed a project, he was

asked to report the results and the method of the study to the class. This was often an invitation for future projects. The reward of recognition had a powerful place in establishing a practice of independent investigation in every class. Team meetings frequently gave serious consideration to ways to encourage interest in independent study. Also, the teachers of several subjects found themselves advising a single student in locating materials for study. Students were encouraged to regard teachers as resources and the youngsters often sought the opinions of different staff members.

Independent study in any form was never used as a punishment. If study was assigned as a response to negative behavior, it could hardly be expected to produce positive feelings toward learning. If punishment was needed, we tried to deny the student the right to work! The faculty established work as a reward and idleness as a penalty. Few adolescents wanted to be denied the right to work or to participate in a group activity. The best approach to negative behavior was to ask the guilty student to leave the group, but not the room, for a specific period. When he returned, he usually improved his behavior. If you question this, try it and see!

Telling Results of Independent Study

Some outstanding independent study projects were developed at Lakeview during the operation of the Decatur-Lakeview Plan. These varied from intricate art work to detailed study of the origin and evolution of law and society. A small group teacher who effectively encouraged independent study could be identified readily by the diversity of independent study activities performed by his students. The students spent evenings and vacations at school working on their independent study projects once they got a "work fever." As students began working on their problems, they often improved the quality of their work.

The Lakeview Instructional Materials Center helped a great deal in making independent study become a reality. Once there was a single place to find diverse materials and the freedom to get them when needed, the quality and quantity of independent study increased.

The teachers of social studies, English, foreign language, and industrial arts found it easier to involve students in independent study than did the other teachers. This was due as much to the acceptance of the worth of independent study as it was to the nature of the content. Science, health, art, homemaking and mathematics teachers were less able to get meaningful independent study activities under way in the beginning of the Plan's operation. However, during the third year of the Plan's development they too joined in the promotion and execution of worthwhile independent study activities. There was less evidence of weighty notebook picture-pasting and poster construction and more evidence of original and creative projects based on detailed study.

An eighth grade social studies student expressed a sentiment held by most of the student body when she commented, "In my independent study time I actually do the learning. The large group sets the stage and gives me topics of interest, and the small group helps me know if I'm on the right track. Most of the real payoff comes from the independent study time."

Some benefit was to be had from joint research projects. The gregarious characteristic of adolescents was exploited in the instructional process and increased learning was the consequence. Some students profited from the stimulation of another student in developing understandings. An outstanding example of this was the work done by three ninth grade girls in studying the effects of climate on dress on each continent of the world from the fifteenth century to modern times. The reading of these girls was tremendous in volume. The procedures they used in gathering materials was astounding for ninth graders. They exhausted local sources, got materials from the state library and wrote to several foreign lands to get background information. The translation of the materials from Germany resulted in a broader understanding of the language and customs.

The general music teacher in the junior high school exploratory courses mentioned to a large group the record collection in the Instructional Materials Center as he explained examples of various kinds of music. The following week the use of the listening stations was so great that a schedule for their use had to be constructed. Interestingly enough, the habit of listening to good music was established for some students as an outgrowth of this one lecture.

Redeployment of Physical and Human Resources for Independent Study

More and more of the school's financial resources had to be spent for the "things" which made it possible to expand individual horizons: equipment, materials, recordings, books, electronic tapes and machines. These were the tools of much independent study. Areas where students could type, construct, record and work together had to be set up.

At Lakeview approximately seventy per cent of the student body used the Instructional Materials Center and the content area laboratories without direct teacher supervision. The other thirty per cent, the faculty felt, profited best from teacher supervision most of the time. Therefore, this group went to assigned areas for teacher-supervised study. The staff goal was to reduce this percentage from thirty to zero.

A set of clearly defined procedures was set up for students who did independent study. Students were not turned loose for independent study, but were given teacher help and the materials to work out their own learning activities. Once again, a considerable amount of staff planning and communication to the student body was necessary before the independent study aspect of the Decatur-Lakeview Plan became fully operative. Teachers were scheduled to the Instructional Materials Center on a regular basis to be available to students when they needed them.

Students who desired to operate freely during their non-class time took a petition to each teacher for signature. The teacher gave no regard to the student's ability in asking the critical question: Would this student profit from independent, self-directed study? If, in the teacher's opinion, the student could work with benefit without close supervision, he signed the petition. If he did not think the student had demonstrated the characteristics of personal responsibility, he did not sign. The petition had to be signed by all the student's small group teachers before he was free to use his independent study time as he wished.

Honor Passes as Another Device

High honor roll students, those who got all "A's," were given an Honor Student pass. This gave them the opportunity to move about with complete freedom. They could attend or not attend lectures and their small group. They had freedom to use any facility at any time, so long as it wasn't already in use. Self-imposed obedience was contrasted to obedience based on threat of punishment in the structure of regulations of independent study. The belief was that some students didn't need to hear a lecture or work in a specific small group. They had already mastered the skills and knowledge under consideration. Such students on these occasions could just as well be doing something of more profit than wasting time on what they already knew.

At the end of the first year the staff almost decided these passes weren't worth the time it took a typist to fill them out because no one ever heard of an honor student not attending a lecture or small group. The students recommended they be continued though, as it was an expression of confidence they appreciated. Therefore, they were still issued after each grading period. In time, these passes began to serve their function, for honor students did spend some of their time in activities other than the regularly scheduled sections.

Established Pattern for Independent Study Use

The petition procedures were devised by both students and staff for two reasons. First, the staff wanted students to regard independent study as a privilege; and, at the same time, the students felt they would be more conscious of their responsibility if they were to ask for it. Second, there was the feeling that benefit would result if a student and teacher discussed whether he or she should or should not have the freedom of the Instructional Materials Center and the laboratories. These frank discussions gave the student a clear picture of the teacher's opinion of him. Also it gave the teacher a further insight into the student's goals, desires and drives. The petitions were one more device to bring students and teachers together to talk about specific student learning behavior.

A student-faculty group (composed of four department heads and five students with the assistant principal as an ex officio member) served as the legislative body for determining procedures for use of inadequate facilities and any other problems of control.

No student with low ability or poor grades was necessarily barred from independent study. Students who didn't have the scholastic ability to get high marks were frequently profitable users of the independent study time and facilities. Interest and self-direction are attributes that students of all abilities have. The pattern of independent study activities was set by each individual pupil. The belief was held that all students, irrespective of ability, would profit from translating their instructional goals into concrete learning experiences.

Independent study was worthwhile in that it made students responsible for their own time, effort and behavior. Without independent study time and activities, the two other learning groups would have been far less effective. In time, the staff noticed a general improvement in the quality of work done because of independent study.

Chapter
Twelve

Facilities Change
and Have New Use

THE school's physical facilities partially determine what can and what cannot be a part of a school's program. Students are directly influenced by the physical features of the school they attend. Therefore, sensitive educators must give careful attention to buildings, furniture and the other instructional facilities.

The facilities—buildings and furniture—and their arrangements, have received too little attention by educators for too long. In shaping a program of instruction serious thought should be given to use of space. A school building in itself cannot dictate what kind of program will go on in a school, but the physical structure can limit the educators' activity. Educators have recently become aware of the truth that space planning is an important educational function.

Any consideration of secondary education must include students, teachers, courses (content), time, and space. To ignore the influence of space or facilities on an educational program is unrealistic in considering the aids or barriers to program improvement. It is not so much the quality of the materials that compose the facility, but the different kinds of space that counts. The thought here is not that the costs of brick and mortar are significant educationally, but that the arrangement and use of "things" affects what students can do. Educational Facilities Laboratories, a non-profit creation of the Ford Foundation, has done a great deal to stimulate research and experimentation on schools' physical problems. Lakeview received a small grant from Educational Facilities Laboratory to do additional planning, to determine space needs of large and small group rooms and to plan for remodeling part of the existing structure.

John Beynon, Educational Facilities Laboratory staff member, worked with the Lakeview administrators on remodeling existing space. Mr. Beynon commented frequently, "It isn't how we've built schoolhouses in the past that is important; it is how we should build them for tomorrow that is critical." Educational programs can be significantly improved by remodeling and rearranging existing buildings.

Team Teaching Needs a Suitable Work Space

If teachers are to work together on instructional problems, an appropriate setting in which they can confer, work with materials or do individual study must be established. It is not uncommon, absurd as it is, to find a school district which gives teachers time to work on course planning and to do professional study, but which does not provide the space for them to use the time profitably.

Prior to the re-employment of three storage rooms, the sectioning off of a corner of the library and the re-use of other space, Lakeview teachers didn't have a specific place to go to work. The establishment of designated and assigned work centers for each teacher stimulated individual and team study and planning. It was mainly on the merits of these makeshift faculty study areas that the building remodeling program included team preparation rooms. Often, makeshift facilities can serve a real purpose in organizational experimentation. As a visiting superintendent commented when surveying the Lakeview plant, "Things are being done here in spite of what you don't have. The re-use of space in less than ideal ways has made it possible to try these ideas with the palaces we so often see in the professional magazines!"

Team Preparation Rooms

The team preparation or teacher office rooms are located next to the Instructional Materials Center. This location brought teachers in close contact with both materials and students. Moreover, the staff found it more convenient to use the store of materials when their work stations or office areas were close to the Instructional Materials Center.

Each team preparation room is equipped with a desk, a file cabinet and a bookcase for every teacher. Thus, there is a feeling of individuality established by the teacher's own equipment for work. The proximity of the other members of the team facilitates team effort.

Visits to other schools with offices for teachers located throughout the building revealed that a communications problem sometimes existed within a staff. Mathematics and social studies teachers used the same workroom, a common hall, a general lounge and came into daily contact with each other in an informal way. From these informal contacts it was pleasing to note the number of worthwhile attitudes and understandings which resulted. Problems can't be identified and solutions can't be proposed without communication. A large school organized in departments sometimes sees the faculty become divided. Pulling the staff together in the same area for planning and working caused one English staff member with ten years of service to remark, "Now we think of the broad implications of our recommendations instead of only considering the effects on the English department."

The team rooms also contained chalk boards and bulletin boards. Some teachers think and explain best with chalk dust on their sleeve. No doors were put on the team rooms so students would never hesitate to seek a teacher's help. The students moved freely between the study carrels in the Instructional Materials Center and the team rooms.

Someday a researcher will isolate the characteristics of a teacher like the advanced mathematics instructor at Lakeview in order to learn why students seek his aid to such a great extent. This man skillfully presents ideas, excites students so they want to learn and then helps them get the job done.

Teachers and Paraprofessional Work Areas

In addition to office space, a functional work area is an essential aid to the teacher. This area should include typewriters, duplicating equipment, transparency production equipment, dictation equipment and other supplies which aid the teacher in transmitting ideas.

At Lakeview a central work area was established rather than a place for various departments to work. In the planning stage it was decided that when paraprofessional time was available the non-certified helpers would be assigned to a pool where they would type, correct papers, prepare slides and do the countless other routine things which do not require a degree in education. Both economy of time and ease of supervision were the reasons for this decision.

One school which has a non-certified worker for each of its larger departments faces a problem of determining an even work load for the secretary. By working through a pool it was felt that cooperative concentration during rush periods would get the job done easier and more satisfactorily. Also, during slack periods, in one department area's production work, another's work could be handled.

The promotion of the pool organization for paraprofessional time was based on the feeling that not all secretarial personnel would be good at the varied tasks which needed attention. For instance, some clerks might have artistic talent and could make transparencies.

During the early stages, when Parent-Teacher Association members and Junior Welfare Association volunteers were the paraprofessionals, it seemed to make more sense for them to go to one place, close to the teacher's office area, to be of full advantage.

Large Group Rooms

How often have we all heard that a school can't try a program of large and small group instruction because "the building isn't built for it!" The Lakeview building wasn't either. It did have a cafeteria and an abandoned World War II temporary building in back of the school used for storage. The cafeteria was rearranged to accommodate two hundred pupils, and the old pre-fab was repaired to house up to ninety pupils. For two years these served very well as the large group areas. When an addition was put on the building, new large group rooms replaced the outbuilding for lectures and the cafeteria was reassigned to use as a cafeteria.

The large group area should be arranged in such a way that the teacher is in the best possible contact with students. This is accomplished by putting the teacher in a corner of the room and arranging seats or tables so there is direct eye contact. The use of the cafeteria meant some students had to sit at an angle from the teacher; but it was ably demonstrated by two years of use that this, although not ideal, is no reason not to attempt a large group program. Facilities, bad as they may be, are seldom a reason not to employ large group instruction. The quality of the instruction is far more important than the room in which it takes place.

A large group room was built with movable walls so the big square area could be divided into four pie-shaped rooms. When the entire space was needed, the walls were pulled back to accommodate up to three hundred students; and when two partitions were together two rooms for one hundred fifty students were available; and when two more partitions were together, four rooms for seventy-five pupils were at hand. The new space was built with maximum flexibility so the organization for instruction could change without being hampered by the inside walls. (See illustration.)

The Transmission Center

To get the full potential of teacher-student communication in the large groups, a transmission center was developed and built for

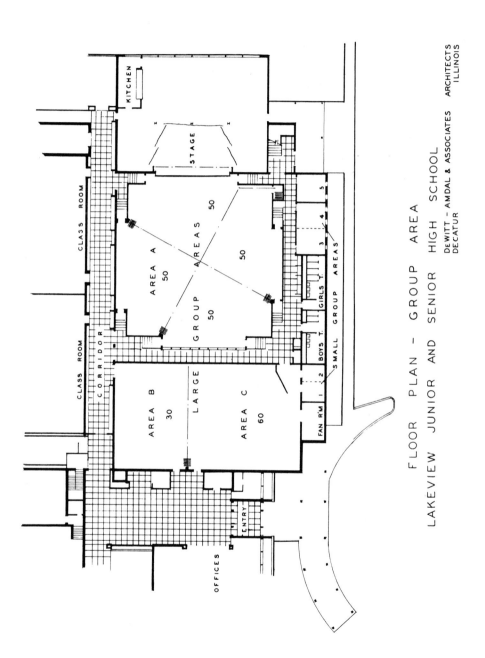

FLOOR   PLAN – GROUP   AREA

LAKEVIEW   JUNIOR   AND   SENIOR   HIGH   SCHOOL

DeWITT – AMDAL & ASSOCIATES   ARCHITECTS
DECATUR   ILLINOIS

each large group area. The transmission center is a large wooden platform, eleven inches off the floor. It houses the amplifier and speaking system so the teacher can speak at normal level and be heard throughout the room. In addition it has a tape recorder built in so that when the speaking system is used, the lecture can be put on a tape. The tape was stored in the Instructional Materials Center for future use by students or the teacher. Some students found it beneficial to use the tapes for review of the content presented in the large group, others found use for the tape when they missed a lecture.

The transmission center also had a phonograph built in for use with the large groups. This too could be hooked into the electronic tape recorder if the teacher desired. In the rear of the platform was a chalk board with a magnetic surface. Teachers could use either the chalk or mock-ups. A large screen located to the right of where the teacher stood pulled down for deflecting the image from the overhead.

The transmission centers have ample storage space for other equipment appropriate for the large groups. A slide projector, sound music projector, opaque projector and flannel material for use over the chalk board are all at hand. This makes it easy for teachers to use learning aids without scheduling problems and lugging machines.

The press of a button on the power switch, the turn of a dial on the amplifier and recorder, the flip of the switch on the overhead and a teacher is ready to hold the attention and appeal to both the senses of sound and sight.

The transmission center was dreamed up in a conference among the administrators and the first model was built in the school district's carpentry shop. Later, after its need was established and its form was perfected, specifications were drawn up and sent out to furniture manufacturers for construction of more centers to satisfy increased needs.

Small Group Rooms

The place where a small group meets, the staff felt, should be one in which communication between each group member is easy. In most content areas Lakeview teachers arrange the desk-tablet chairs in a circle. This makes it possible for any member of the group to see all others in the group. Often communication takes place in the classroom without a word being spoken through glances, facial expressions, etc.

The social studies teachers recommended trapezoidal tables for their small groups. They felt students did a better job of discussing ideas when the group was unified by a common table and when everyone, teacher included, sat facing each other at a relatively close distance.

Some small group rooms demand specialized facilities. Science classes for instance, need equipment, reference work, and charts at hand. By and large the small group rooms were not used by only one particular content group.

The Laboratories for Learning

Special learning laboratories had to be established to give opportunity and space for students to actually do independent study projects and work. Specialized facilities were set up in the following areas:

Art—A room for working with all the media with plenty of storage space was established.

Business Education—Carrels and small rooms equipped with typewriters for practice were established. Carrels with good-sized tops are used for bookkeeping. A special room contained all the business machines. (This facility is used both for small group instruction and for independent study.)

English—The Instructional Materials Center has a room devoted to materials used in English classes. Carrels are adjacent to this.

Foreign Language—A thirty-six position listen, respond and record Language Laboratory is used for independent study by all language students.

Homemaking—Both sewing and foods preparation areas are available for independent study.

Industrial Arts—A general shop serves this area. A separate drawing room is used for the independent study in drafting and architectural drawing.

Mathematics—Study carrels in the Instructional Materials Center serve this content area.

Music—Six listening rooms and instrumental practice space are a part of the music department's learning laboratories.

Physical Education—The gym is set up with areas for use in independent laboratory problems.

Science—Special rooms are set up for physical, biological and chemical science work.

Social Studies—A large room is included in the Instructional Materials Center for reading, writing, viewing and listening with social science materials.

Each teacher worked out recommendations for rooms, equipment and materials for use in independent study work. The materials and equipment which could be used by several content areas were put in the Instructional Materials Center. Some learning laboratories were specialized, like the language laboratory, and therefore required separate housing. Every attempt was made to make equipment and materials as accessible and as easy to use as possible. The center of all the independent study activities was the Instructional Materials Center, the most important facility in the school.

Furniture

Furniture is worth more consideration than school people have given it in the past. Generally, we say a library—or wherever the major storage area of books resides—is a place for quiet study. Yet, a tendency persists to put furniture which facilitates noise in such quiet zones. A rectangular table for six or more students invites communication. Why, then, do these tables find a place in a library reading area? On the other hand, in classrooms we say we want students to ask questions, to speak out in discussion and for recitation, and yet we arrange learners in single chairs placed in rows in which a discussant's view is directed to the back of the head of the person in front of him. There is good reason to take the single chairs out of the classrooms and replace them with tables, which are aids to communication; and take the tables out of the study area and replace them with single-person reading tables.

Consideration has been given at Lakeview to room furnishings. Each content area teacher has been asked to study the kind of furniture which will increase student effectiveness in the content areas. Therefore, the mathematics room has an arrangement different from that of the English room. The mathematics teachers have students seated in pairs at rectangular tables. The purpose is to encourage students to check their applications of process with each other. In the English room the furniture is tablet armchairs arranged in a circle, allowing either group or individual work. In the business education department trapezoidal tables are employed to make discussion and workbook study possible.

The Concern in Facility Use: Learning Stimulation

Each course or cluster of courses has different space and facility needs. When a course is planned it behooves the planner to be mindful of the furniture and facility needs. The central concern should be this: how can space and furniture stimulate and facilitate learning?

It is important to have adequate facilities but even more important that their location or relationship to one another is vital. There was merit, the staff felt, in putting the several science or mathematics rooms close together. Also, it is wise to put teachers' offices in a cluster, thus encouraging the interchange of ideas among teachers and facilitating student-teacher communication outside of class.

Anyone responsible for planning school facilities, the Lakeview administrators felt, should keep in mind the changing nature of the curriculum and instructional methods. A schoolhouse should be a solid shell with flexible internal parts so that the arrangement of space is not an obstruction to the educational program's changes. Buildings should be planned and built, then, in such a way that change in instructional program can be made without great expense or waste. Load-bearing walls are a monument to the past. Today wise school builders construct schools which are flexible and adaptable. The needs of this decade aren't necessarily those of the next. School structures should be put together in such a way that they can be rearranged to meet the needs of a different era. There is truth in the old saying that one generation builds a school and four more suffer consequences. Planning should provide for future adjustments.

The Decatur architects, DeWitt-Amdal and Associates, did a

superior job in keeping the Decatur-Lakeview Plan's program solidly in mind and in following the educational specifications in the re-modeling and building addition program. School architects should understand educational aims before they take pencil and ruler in hand. Educators would do well to get an L.Q. (listening quotient) on each architectural firm being considered for employment. DeWitt-Amdal and Associates created a windowless Instructional Materials Center which was larger than the school's gymnasium. They developed a large group room with marble walls and designed Lakeview's significant resource areas for both staff and student study.

The Instructional Materials Center

Schools are beginning to match *doing* with *knowing*. A manifesta-tion of this is the establishment of Instructional Materials Centers in secondary schools. The Decatur-Lakeview Plan demanded the estab-lishment of an Instructional Materials Center. When students were given a block of time for independent study, they needed a place filled with materials to help them carry out their individual work. The belief that successful learning is the result of directed activity implied the need for a place for students to be able to read, to view, to listen and to construct.

The Instructional Materials Center at Lakeview was a place where "ideas" were housed. The Instructional Materials Center (I.M.C.) contained books, magazines, pamphlets, pictures, films, film strips, tapes, slides, recordings, transparencies, mock-ups and learning programs. An accurate description of the I.M.C. is clouded if its functions are not defined. Basically, the I.M.C. is a resource center for ideas to be transmitted by materials and teaching tools. It is a place where students work when not in a formal class. Teachers use it in selecting learning experiences and students use it in carrying out the teacher-directed activities, as well as for independent study.

The Characteristics of the Materials Center

The organization of materials was a clue to the functions of the professional and paraprofessional I.M.C. workers. For teachers, the director (a professional librarian with audio-visual aids interest and training) and all other staff served as resource-gathering helpers in learning experience construction. For students the persons assigned to the I.M.C. were consultants and resource advisors. There has been a recurring practice from the Middle Ages in the use of resources in our schools. In the days when books were reproduced by the scribes, reference materials often were bolted down to the tables, for they were to be used by only a select few. Some schools have continued to guard materials as if they should not be accessible to all. Twentieth century technology has made it possible to reproduce materials in gigantic volume. The I.M.C. was a place where all the tools of learning could be used by students. Therefore, it was more than a storage center. It was a busy, active work center. The stacks were open; listening and viewing rooms were fully equipped and easily available. Skilled guidance by the Center staff was necessary for optimum usefulness, however, if the diverse materials were to be employed fully. Having all the resources in the world isn't worthwhile without a staff that actually encourages their use.

Like a library, the I.M.C. had reading spaces in a "quiet zone"; but it also had a place for typing, conferring, viewing, listening and working in a "noise zone." There were carrels, independent study spaces for an individual, as well as small group or conference rooms.

Too often in the past, schools have been organized in such a way that the audio-visual "department" had one center of interest and the library "department" another. Such a division implies a difference in their place in the learning process. Also, ease of use of these materials is a cornerstone of the I.M.C. To insure this the doors of the Lakeview I.M.C. were left off conference, book storage and audio-visual storage rooms. Accessibility and freedom characterized the Instructional Materials Center.

Much of the actual learning that students did was accomplished as a result of what went on in a class activity, but not directly by the class activity itself. The stirring lecture and the stimulating discussion contributed to the desire for additional knowledge of many students. It was in the I.M.C. that out-of-class but class-related activities were carried out by the student.

The Ease of Use of the Materials Center

The physical design and the materials on hand were important in the Instructional Materials Center. "Things" were sometimes necessary for ideas to be explored and understood. Therefore, a storehouse of teaching aids was established. It included models, prototypes, puzzles and so forth. There had to be the recognition that diverse and uninterrupted activities *would* and *should* go on in the operating Instructional Materials Center. Thus, quiet zones for some work and noise zones for other work were needed.

Service was the keyword in the I.M.C.—service to both students and teachers. The staff of the Center accepted this role and sought to cultivate an understanding of the needs of the various content areas within the school. This implied ample and frequent communication between teachers and the director of the Center. Such communication was not left to chance. Regular procedures and conferences had to be set up whereby a two-way flow of ideas passed between teachers and the staff of the Center. Often department or teacher meetings were devoted to this at Lakeview. In addition, grade level or content area meetings scheduled three times a year were helpful in involving the teachers in materials selection and in allowing the director to call teachers' attention to recent acquisitions and student problems in using materials.

A great many Lakeview classes have found advantage in meeting in the Center rather than in a classroom. Teachers thereby gave valuable aid by giving students firsthand help in finding and using resource materials.

The I.M.C. can be elaborate and inclusive of many specialized materials for varied activities or it can be limited in content and form. The most elaborate part of the Lakeview building was the Instructional Materials Center. The latter was testimony to this staff's belief in its worth and place in the school's program. (See illustration.)

The Place of the Center Is Prominent

Excellent content presentation does not necessarily insure effec-

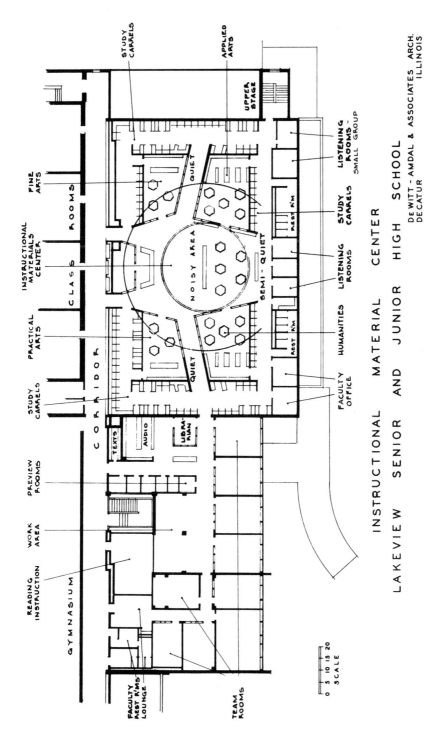

INSTRUCTIONAL MATERIAL CENTER

LAKEVIEW SENIOR AND JUNIOR HIGH SCHOOL

DE WITT - AMDAL & ASSOCIATES ARCH.
DECATUR ILLINOIS

145

tive learning. Not only does the capable teacher know this, but the viewer of a television extravaganza understands it when pressed to report in detail what happened on a carefully prepared and rehearsed television show. Seeing a network's finest presentation of the life of Lincoln, for example, doesn't insure our appreciation of the man's worth or our mastery of the facts concerning his life. We learn best when we use and arrange facts and ideas. The I.M.C. was the place where this use and arrangement of ideas and facts could take place by students.

The teaching staff at Lakeview used this Center in designing learning experiences and in developing methods of instruction. The master teacher purposefully encouraged students to use varied sources and seek divergent views. The lectures at Lakeview often mentioned source material in the Center for student reference. Before a teacher could encourage others to use the Center, he himself had to be aware of what was available, and he had to suggest additions that he thought necessary. Staff members had to be regularly involved in the selection of learning materials. There was real value in having teachers work in the same physical area as students, for by this means teaching was done by example, as well as by direction. Also, students were easily able to seek a teacher's aid when he was working beside the student in the Center.

Within recent years a vast amount of new instructional materials have been developed. In business education, there are a number of excellent tapes which students can use to improve shorthand skill. Recordings of many aspects of social studies have been made to strengthen instruction in this area. A student, for example, cannot help but gain in understanding of the racial problem after having listened to the commercial recordings of the Nashville sit-in strikes. Architectural drafting students can learn techniques of their art by the use of special transparencies illustrating theories of design. Poetry is more than rhyme and meter when one hears Dylan Thomas read his own poems. Mathematics understanding can be aided by the use of programmed learning materials. These are only a few examples of the kinds of materials which can strengthen skills and add to content knowledge.

The Card Catalog Is All Inclusive

The nerve center of the I.M.C. is the central catalog, a road map of the endless paths to understanding. Here everything related to a topic is identified for the user. For instance, books may be catalogued on white cards, films on blue cards, film strips on green, and transparencies on yellow cards. This means that when the student wants to locate all the information about World War II, for instance, he will have a chance to consider the use of books, maps, films, tapes of lectures, magazines, etc.

Some schools have found it beneficial to have the school's catalog cross-referenced with the public library, for this gives direction to additional information. The Lakeview card catalog had a reference to all materials stored in the central office audio-visual center. These materials were used as never before because of this simple technique of adding them to the building card catalog. Teachers could find at a glance all the resources at hand in the school system.

The Organization of Materials and Assistance in Use

Two approaches are used in making the materials available. Some schools house all related materials in the same room; others house the items by classification. That is, some put films on the shelf next to books, and others have a separate house for each kind of material. Facilities and personnel preference govern the decision as to which is better. The Lakeview decision was to store them in separate rooms indexed by the general catalog.

Even items not housed in the I.M.C., but found in other rooms in the school, should be included in the general card catalog. For example, if a school has a mock-up of a heart housed in a biology room, it should be included in the I.M.C. catalog with a note indicating that the mock-up is on loan to the biology room. This points the way to its use by students who are interested in the heart, but who are not biology students. During the non-teaching part of the day, some schools may want to schedule content area teachers to the I.M.C. to answer questions of students in their field. Here the consultation with several teachers is cited for the same reasons that the use of multiple texts is advocated. Diversity of approach and difference in explanation often strengthens a student's understanding of content.

The director must know a great deal about the student population. He must know what is needed—books, transparencies, maps, magazines, films, etc. He needs to exercise judgment in selecting materials in order to keep a balance that will result in integrated learning experiences. The Center contains materials for use by students—rulers, typewriters, paper punches, transparency production equipment, paste—and numerous other "tools" for instruction.

The Freedom to Use the Center

The practice of requiring a "pass" or "permit" to go to the Center is obnoxious to the basic concept of the I.M.C. Freedom to seek, ease to use, and encouragement to find are the foundations of this important area of the school. We have found that if students are given more real freedom to pursue diverse activities, there are fewer student control problems. The point is this: Let the readers read; let the non-readers listen; let the notebook constructors paste, cut and arrange. By presenting various opportunities, we are enabling students to find methods best suited to their learning abilities. If a minority in a school population cannot profit from such freedom, there is no reason to set up rules which restrict the majority.

A Commitment Is Basic to the Center's Operation

As with all ideas that cause people to change their method of operation, it is required that there be an intellectual acceptance of the basic concepts of the Instructional Materials Center on the part of the staff. This is not done by administrative edict or physical rearrangement. Teachers need to be involved in contributing ideas for this agency's operation, as well as in the materials acquisition. Existing sub-libraries need to be integrated in the new Instructional Materials Center and encouragement must be given in order for teachers to want to use it.

Too frequently, administrators fail to recognize their role in improving instruction by establishing new programs or procedures. The Instructional Materials Center won't just grow like Topsy. It needs attention and care if it is to grow and mature. Once established, frequent reference should be made to it, and continual evaluation should be made of its use by students and faculty.

The Instructional Materials Center is a promise for progress if faithfully used. It is the manifestation of the belief that "individuals" are taught and not "subjects." Like all theories, however, it is no better than its functional application.

Part Three

Experience Has a Lesson

The conditions that direct the order of the living world are marked by their persistence in improving the birthright of successive generations. They determine, at much cost of individual comfort, that each plant and animal shall, on the general average, be endowed at its birth with some more suitable natural facilities than those of its representative in the preceding generation.

Francis Galton

Chapter
Thirteen

The Student
in the Decatur-Lakeview Plan

S INCE Lakeview High School served students from grades
seven through twelve, it was necessary to consider the
needs of learners of various stages of maturation and experience. It was decided immediately that what was good for a
timid seventh grade youngster wasn't always best for an independent twelfth grade young adult. More frequently than
not the converse was true.

It was thought that the differences were in degree and
not kind. That is, the instructional prescription for a junior
high age youngster needed to vary from that for the older,
more experienced, more mature student in terms of depth,
duration and intensity. Common agreement was found on
how people—regardless of age—learn. The Decatur-Lakeview Plan was built on a theory of learning with application

to people; but it was to be applied in different ways, for varying lengths of time and at graded levels, for students of the several age levels included in the junior-senior high school.

Questions Most Frequently Asked About Students

Visitors to the Lakeview School frequently asked questions about the pupils' behavior in the large groups, their use or abuse of independent study and their willingness to be active participants in the small groups. Another matter of concern to professional observers was how well students did on achievement tests which were standardized on national norms.

A careful check of the behavior problems with the assistant principal, the one responsible for irregular discipline problems, was kept prior to the Plan's inauguration and after it was in operation. It was substantiated by experience that fewer discipline cases were sent to the assistant principal after the Plan was in operation than before. The assistant principal commented at the end of the first year of the Plan's operation, "I have been more of an educator and less of a disciplinarian this year. The demand for the devil's advocate decreased to make this possible."

In the year-end evaluations made by the staff there was a pronounced sentiment that the general discipline of the school was improved as a result of the Decatur-Lakeview Plan. This, in itself, was felt to be a great advantage of the Plan by some staff members. As the philosophy of putting more responsibility on the learner to learn became a practice, an improved climate for learning was established. Normal adolescent desires for activity, for energy release and for idea testing were provided in the structure of the Decatur-Lakeview Plan's small group work and independent study.

By and large, the student body of Lakeview profited from independent study privileges. The measure of the success of this part of the school day was in the positive results noted in studies which students made of various topics. In English, for instance, the quality of work done by the freshmen in creative writing far surpassed the work which came from students in traditional do-alike classes on an advanced grade level. In social studies it became the standard practice of inquiry to consult diverse references in contrast to using the single text for everything.

Students can be freed from single-track thinking by encouraging them to delve into multiple sources. The development of an affection for inquiry was as much a goal of instruction as the aim of covering subject matter. Once students succumbed to the spirit and used the process of inquiry, the productive aspect of learning began. Students started to ask more "Why" questions. When this happened, the Plan was improving.

While it was true that a few students wasted some of their time during the part of the day set aside for independent study, it was also true that those same students would not be fully productive during all of the day in a school organized in a traditional manner. The human machine doesn't operate at its highest level all the time, regardless of the environment or motivation! Too often we forget that.

The organizational pattern of a school did not guarantee how students would function, but it did open some new avenues of learning and discouraged other kinds of less valuable motion. The Decatur-Lakeview Plan freed students for independent study to a degree not often possible in a traditional arrangement. With the high quality presentations possible in the large group and the close student-teacher relationship in the small group, the student was given both motivation and assistance in learning. What more could any school do?

Subject Mastery and Student Involvement

It was significant to note how intrigued visitors to the Lakeview school were as they observed youngsters actively performing in the small group. The difference between the extent and quality of participation in a small group and a traditional class was pronounced.

If there is a doubt in your mind about the possibility of getting real student-centered classes, the only thing we can say is, try it and you'll see! Students do enjoy being engaged in small group work. Admittedly, it takes time to get these enterprises going. A skillful teacher needs to be on hand to manipulate content and to move in and out of the class activity as needed.

A careful analysis of the achievement tests given Lakeview students clearly demonstrated that the students had assimilated as much subject matter as could be expected in relation to their ability. That is, group norms on achievement tests were highly correlated with the norms on aptitude tests. The testing program results gave strength to the belief that students were doing well in terms of measured learning products. Of course, the aim of the program was to develop a high "Quest Quotient," as Frank Brown, the provocative Florida principal, refers to that desire that separates a seeking, thoughtful man from a knowing, knowledgeable man.

Learning products, as measured by standardized achievement tests, were more easily measured than the qualities of intellectual interest, self-realization and creative talent which the Plan hoped to promote. The staff evaluation of the instructional program in relation to student educational progress was most vital. As the table below shows, the staff felt at the conclusion of the second year that students were doing well and getting their full measure of content with the Decatur-Lakeview Plan.

FACULTY EVALUATION SUMMARY			
Compared to previous years, students are learning content to a degree which is:	42	12	3	2
	More	Same	Less	Don't Know
Compared to previous years, students are doing outside of class activity which is:	48	6	1	2
	Higher Quality	Same Quality	Lower Quality	Don't Know
Compared to previous years, students are covering material in depth to a degree which is:	43	7	0	7
	Increased	Same	Decreased	Don't Know

The faculty evaluation, measured by opinionnaires twice each year, repeatedly verified the proposition that students learn as much if not more with the Decatur-Lakeview Plan. In addition, the staff members noticed an improved attitude toward learning.

Appendix II reports the students' evaluation of the Decatur-

Lakeview Plan. Other, less formal, evaluations were made from time to time.

Module	Monday	Tuesday	Wednesday	Thursday	Friday
1	Engl. (L.G.)	Wld. Hist. (S.G.)	Engl. (L.G.)	Wld. Hist. (S.G.)	Engl. (L.G.)
2	Indep. St.		Pl. Geom. (S.G.)		French (S.G.)
3		French (L.G.)		French (L.L.)	
4	Typing (S.G.)	Phys. Ed. (L.G.)	Indep. St.	Phys. Ed. (L.G.)	English (S.G.)
5	Phys. Educ.	Indep. St.		Indep. St.	
6					Indep. St.
7	Lunch	Dr. Ed. (L.G.)	Typing (S.G.)	Lunch	
8	French (S.G.)	Lunch	Lunch	French (L.G.)	Lunch
9		Pl.Geom.(L.G.)	Wld. Hist. (S.G.)	Pl.Geom.(L.G.)	Indep. St.
10	Indep. St.	Indep. St.		Indep. St.	
11			Indep. St.		Soph. Cl. Act.
12	Wld. Hist. (S.G.)	English (S.G.)		English (S.G.)	Wld. Hist. (S.G.)
13			Dr. Ed. (S.G.)		
14	Pl. Geom. (S.G.)	Indep. St.	French (S.G.)	Indep. St.	Pl. Geom. (S.G.)
15					

L.G.—Large Group   Indep. St.—Independent Study
S.G.—Small Group   L.L.—Language Laboratory

This student's schedule can be visualized another way. In terms of learning groups, this schedule would constitute:

Large Groups	Small Groups	Independent Study
English—3	English—3	as selected by student
Driver Education—1	Driver Education—1	as selected by student
French—2	French—3	Language Laboratory—1
Physical Education—2	Physical Education—2	as selected by student
Plane Geometry—2	Plane Geometry—3	as selected by student
Typing—0	Typing—2	as selected by student
World History—3	World History—2	as selected by student
Sophomore Class Act.—1		

Each of the above large groups lasted for twenty-seven minutes, each of the small groups for at least fifty-seven minutes. The independent study time was allocated on the basis of the student's need.

Students taking laboratory courses, art, science, homemaking and industrial arts, had their class schedule arranged so they met for an hour and a half or two hours in these subjects. They usually met two or sometimes three days a week in small groups, as well as in large groups—depending on the content demands. Some courses, like typing, met for only two formal classes a week, but students were given skill development work to do as the staff saw fit. Business education teachers were in the Instructional Materials Center area to give assistance as it was needed, for instance, in typing, bookkeeping, business law and so forth.

The Student's Role Changed

Students needed to be left on their own to work, but professional aid had to be at hand when required by the students. Teachers were viewed through different eyes by students once the staff members became resource people who satisfied students' needs. This new relationship between teacher and student was a healthy one, satisfying both to student and teacher. In the traditional situation the teacher's role was that of the seeker; the student's was that of the sought. The Decatur-Lakeview Plan attempted to reverse these roles.

By reducing the amount of direct staff supervision in content explanation and skill mastery the roles were gradually reversed. A typical reaction to this relationship was expressed by a junior girl when she said, "Lakeview teachers are interested in each of us. Rather than questioning us about what they want, we question them about what we need to understand." The small group teachers helped students realize their instructional needs.

At least two staff members were available for assistance to students during each module of the day. The team planning offices were built next to the Instructional Materials Center so students would have easy access to teachers.

The flexible program implied a rearrangement of students in learning groups. When a youngster wasn't profiting from a course or a group in his mind and/or in his teacher's, there was little hesitation to make section changes. Students who learned easily and well were relieved of some elementary courses or sections and students of low ability were not required to stay in normative groups. The criterion was what was best for the student.

Students Grasped the Plan

The student body grasped the purposes and procedures of the Decatur-Lakeview Plan. They were well aware of what was going on and why the school was organized as it was. It was startling at first to a visitor to hear students talking about their school in the lingo of Lakeview. The conversation went something like this:

MIKE: "I have a project committee meeting the tenth module in the I.M.C. so I can't see you in the viewing rooms." (This means that Mike is working with several other students for a half-hour immediately after lunch on a problem which came from a small group class. He will meet with another student in a conference room off of the Instructional Materials Center and, therefore, can't look at a film in the special viewing room then.)

SALLY: "Your evaluation of my independent study project would be helpful. Why don't you stop by the listening center at the end of the twelfth module or by the student service area the end of the fourteenth module? I want to see if you agree with the Teacher Presenter on his thesis." (Sally was asking for a value judgment after she'd completed a paper. She will be listening to tapes of lectures given previously for review purposes during part of the afternoon. Then she'll be in the student work area doing some duplicating. She wanted a comment on the concept presented in a large group by the teacher with lecture responsibilities.)

And so the day went! Students took to these new procedures with ease and enthusiasm. The structure of the school facilitated learning by means of the large and small groups with independent study. Students found this out and adapted to it quickly.

Lakeview students didn't have a great deal of difficulty in remembering their schedules. New students were given help, but such aid is necessary for any youngster new to a school. Somehow the variability of the interest caused students to be conscious of their schedules.

Implementation Procedures

So that students would have insight into the reasons for the Decatur-Lakeview Plan and so that they would have a crystal-clear understanding of the new procedures, a number of steps were taken to communicate with students about the Plan's operation. It was thought that as much discussion as possible should go on before the Plan was started so that the desired behavior change in students would occur with as much speed as possible.

Once the staff commitment was sealed, the program of student education began. The Student Council officers met with the principal to discuss the program of orienting the students. The Student Council officers agreed to hold several meetings on the rationale of the Plan. In time the class representatives reported these to all the students. Panels were set up to discuss the various sizes of groups, the changing role of students and teachers, the opportunities for increased educational opportunity and other aspects of the Plan.

Group guidance class discussions were centered on the new program the spring before it was inaugurated on an all-school basis. Students knew something of the large and small groups since they had been tried in several content areas. Teachers in all departments began employing some elements of the Plan during the semester before it went into full operation. The idea was to bring about gradual changes in procedures on a one-by-one, one change with one group, basis before combining all the pieces into the Plan. This principle of gradualism seemed to be worthwhile. Teachers learned from their exploratory experiences. Students were pleased with the original adjustments and anticipated the full-scale change.

Decision-making on the students' part gradually came in line with the philosophical base of the school. For example, the Student Council pushed for opening the library in the evening so students could pursue their work in the atmosphere of the school. While this wasn't approved as a standard procedure by the central office administration, it was a sign of the direction in which the students wanted to go.

Each edition of the school newspaper carried an article explaining one aspect of the Plan. Experience taught us that both students and parents read the newspaper. Parents sometimes got a glimpse of the school through a discarded school paper that they didn't get in dinner-time conversations.

As the news of the Decatur-Lakeview Plan was carried by the local newspaper and television station, student interest increased. Somehow students took increased pride in their school when it was noticed by others. This is an instance in which the Hawthorne Effect had distinct operational advantage. Having noticed this outcome in the beginning, we worked to maintain a successive series of Hawthorne-creating events. As long as the changes were actual, concrete, and beneficial, we did not hesitate to discuss them in any media.

Discussion of the Plan with students was necessarily unending. When the discourse between administrators and students ceases, the program will die. The Decatur-Lakeview Plan was based on the needs of the Lakeview students to increase content mastery and skill development through better use of teacher talent and student time. Emphasis was put on independent responsibility for learning. As the program is in operation over the years, it is assumed it will be refined in relation to its fundamental aim: quality instruction for each new generation of adolescents. A school administrator needs to keep in tune with the times and adjust the school program to benefit each group of scholars. Each time the population of a school changes, so should the school program. It is the administrative function to assist the staff in gearing the school program to the student needs.

Student Evaluation of the Plan

Students were asked twice each year, once in late October and once in early May, to evaluate the Decatur-Lakeview Plan. The purpose of the opinionnaire was to keep track of attitudes concerning the Plan with the hope of learning of weak spots.

Informal discussions with students revealed real satisfaction with the philosophical framework and its application. It is significant to note, however, that students who were tardy with their work blamed the Plan. On the other hand, students with low achievement were not always ready to blame the Plan. Quite to the contrary, they expressed satisfaction with the school's organization in spite of their own scholastic disability. It seemed that the staff did a superior job of giving all levels of learners a feeling of success and personal worth.

By the end of the second year four evaluations had been made of the Decatur-Lakeview Plan by the students. They were positive in their general tone and constant on the strengths of the Plan. It was encouraging to know that the students continued to have positive attitudes toward the Decatur-Lakeview Plan, for these evaluations were taken very seriously by the staff.

STUDENT EVALUATION SUMMARY, SECOND YEAR COMPOSITE		
Statement	*Response*	
I feel I profit from the Decatur-Lakeview Plan.	Yes—83% No — 6%	Don't Know—9% No Answer—2%
I feel I would learn more if I were in a class of 25 meeting once each day.	Yes— 4% No —88%	Don't Know—7% No Answer—1%
I believe I am learning as much as or more than I would with a traditional school organization.	Yes—91% No — 6%	Don't Know—3% No Answer—0%
Check the learning group you feel is the most helpful to you.	Large Group—38% Small Group—44%	Traditional Group— 4% Independent Study—14%
Please rate your adjustment to more than one teacher in a single course.	Easy— 81% Difficult—15%	No Reaction—4% No Answer— 0%

Graduates' Reaction to the Plan

Students attending colleges reported they had little difficulty in adjusting. Those graduates who did not do well in a college or university had personal adjustment problems and, more than likely, would not have mastered college life or college work regardless of their high school program.

The terminal students reported they did well on their jobs and, a follow-up survey indicated, felt the high school program suited them for their post-high-school work. They had some constructive suggestions to make relating to increased emphasis on the acquisition of materials, especially audio, for the Instructional Materials Center.

Both college-bound and terminal graduates expressed a feeling of satisfaction with the program and strongly recommended that it be continued. One graduate summed up the feeling of many of his classmates this way: "When I was at Lakeview, it was just school. I heard it was different; now I know it was better. As I talk with other high school graduates, I appreciate the fact that they were given instruction—and we learned."

Chapter
Fourteen

The Teacher Is Vital to the Decatur-Lakeview Plan

*T*HE *greatest asset of any school is its professional staff.*
Critics may be right when they point out how teaching
talent is abused in today's schools. That is, professional educators are too frequently asked to perform functions which are
not commensurate with their skill or ability. Money-collecting,
typing, cafeteria supervision and countless other menial tasks
have, unfortunately, become a part of a teacher's job. Too
often the evaluation of teachers is related to these non-teaching chores. The time will surely come when we can reserve
teachers for teaching and bring another person, the skilled
paraprofessional worker, into the schools to handle the non-
technical and clerical details of teaching.

The goal of the Lakeview staff was to develop a program
of maximum utilization of teaching talent and time. While

the housekeeping functions were recognized as vital to the daily operation of the school, new ways were sought to discharge them and thereby to improve effectiveness of every teacher. Also, the assumptions were made that, one, as teachers decreased the range of their function, they would increase their proficiency in the area of concentration; and, two, that increased personal satisfaction would accrue to the teacher as his skill was refined and his teaching responsibility was expanded. Said another way, as teachers get more delight from centering their attention on the teaching-learning process, the quality of education should increase.

A further transgression on the talent of teachers is the expectation that the teacher can concentrate on those parts of the teaching process. Although some teachers are expert at content presentation, for example, it doesn't necessarily follow that they are equally competent at test construction or at giving individualized learning prescriptions. Each step in the teaching process is dependent on the other. Students need good content presentations, knowledge of diverse resources, appropriate learning experience activities, adequate evaluation and personal assistance. Regardless of where the teacher's interest lies, the student has the right to expect the very best he can receive at each of these.

The need for specialization exists in the teaching profession so that the teacher can concentrate on those parts of the teaching process at which he is the most highly skilled and best trained to perform. Teacher-training programs need to sharpen their focus on those aspects of the science of instruction which can be improved through training. Specialists need to be developed in curriculum planning, content presentation, learning experience selection and in the other phases of instruction. The purpose of specialization of the teaching role is to increase the quality of the contacts students have in the teaching-learning process. As the teacher narrows the range of teaching functions, improved quality is likely to result from those operations on which his interest is centered.

The Lakeview Approach to Specialization of Function

A number of studies have been made over the past dozen years on the isolation of elements in the teaching process. More are needed.

These were carefully reviewed by the Lakeview staff, who felt a need to study functions of the teaching process to see where it might be logical to arrange clusters of tasks. These clusters would then represent a teaching speciality or assignment.

Two broad areas of teaching responsibility were defined. One was centered around content and its presentation and coordination. The other centered upon functions related to direct student-teacher interaction. The other functions in the teaching process were considered to be non-professional in nature and could be performed by a non-certified person.

The first group of tasks, those related to content, were assigned to a person called the Teacher Presenter. This member of the teaching team would:

1. Serve as chairman of the teaching team.

2. Plan methods of and make the presentation.

3. Carry on the research and study necessary for getting the proper depth and breadth of content for the course.

4. Be responsible for over-all course evaluation.

5. Work with the Teacher Leader(s) in team efforts.

The second member of the team would work with students after the Teacher Presenter had performed the content presentation function. This person was called the Teacher Leader and this specialist would:

1. Work directly with the small groups.

2. Help individual students with their specific learning problems.

3. Be responsible for student evaluation.

4. Participate in team planning and decision-making.

While the roles were being defined it was obvious the staff did not want the definition to become so narrow that a breach would develop between the Teacher Presenter and the Teacher Leader. That is, the demand for a free flow of communication between the two roles was obvious. The responsibilities for coordination of effort and planning were built into each role specification through the teaching teams.

Countless hours of heated discussion went into the decision to divide teaching tasks between the two roles. Although another level or area of professional worker was considered and envisioned, one to work only with students in independent study, it seemed inappropriate during the early development of the Decatur-Lakeview Plan. The staff felt the time would come when some certified teachers would work exclusively with students in a one-to-one relationship on an *ad hoc* basis.

AN ANATOMY OF THE TEACHING PROCESS	
Function	*Responsibility*
Content Selection	Team Effort
Preparing Multimedia Aids	Teacher Presenter
Content Presentation	Teacher Presenter
Lesson Planning	Teacher Leader
Group Planning	Teacher Leader
Learning Experience Selection (All Students)	Teacher Presenter
Learning Experience Selection (Individual Students)	Teacher Leader
Assignment Correction	Teacher Leader
Test Construction	Team Effort
Course Evaluation	Team Effort
Student Evaluation	Teacher Leader
Coordinating Team Activities	Teacher Presenter

Owing to the size of the Lakeview School population, few teachers had only large groups. Usually teachers lectured in several areas or in different content departments. Some Teacher Presenters used a small group assignment as a gauge of how the content was being received from the large groups. This had the advantage, at the beginning anyway, of giving all the team members an idea of the problems to be confronted.

The Distribution of Staff Time

Once the general agreement was reached about the definition of each member of the teaching team, decisions needed to be made about the distribution of time needed for preparation, for team planning and for professional study. It was noticed at the outset that a different amount of time was required for the various members of the teaching team.

It was generally agreed that preparation for a small group would not be extensive if the enterprise was to be a student-centered activity. How could one plan for student questions or student needs? Some time was needed by the small group teacher, the Teacher Leader, for correcting papers and doing research work in the Instructional Materials Center. It was agreed that two modules, or approximately an average of one hour a day, was sufficient.

In addition it was decided the Teacher Leader needed to have a meeting at least two days a week with the Teacher Presenter. These meetings were of various lengths, depending on the department and the course. By and large, the skill subjects did not demand as many team meetings as the subject-matter courses. Most teams were scheduled for four modules of common meeting time each week. This meant a Teacher Leader would have fourteen modules or seven clock hours of non-student contact time each week. This was contrasted with the usual preparation time of twenty modules or ten hours of released time given teachers in the traditional schedule of five classes and two preparation periods each day. Therefore, the Teacher Leaders could assume more student contact hours in a week than a teacher working in a traditional schedule.

The Teacher Presenter's role included the demand for increased non-student contact time for preparation of lectures, test construction and for research and study. We wanted well-prepared lectures and we had to give time to make this a reality. Since the number of lectures varied in the different courses, a common formula couldn't be established for all Teacher Presenters. The preparation time needed depended on the number of lectures to be given. The formula agreed upon was two modules of preparation for all Presenters and two additional modules for each module of assigned large groups. In addition, the team meeting time, at least two meetings of four modules or two hours each week, was deducted from the student contact time. Also, each Teacher Presenter was given two hours or four modules of time for visiting small groups or for additional research work on evaluation of the course content and progress. Visiting small groups was thought to be important in order for the Teacher Presenter to know how students were assimilating the content.

It was agreed that when non-certified people were added they would work fifteen modules or seven and a half hours a day.

NON-STUDENT CONTACT TIME FORMULA		
Role	*Purpose*	*Time*
Teacher Leader	Preparation	2 modules each day
All Team Members	Planning	4 modules each week (scheduled together)
Teacher Presenter	Preparation	2 modules for each large group meeting each day
Teacher Presenter	Research, Evaluation	2 modules each day

Translated into student contact time, this meant the Teacher Leader was meeting with students fifty-six modules or roughly twenty-eight hours a week. The Teacher Presenters, on an average, were meeting with students twenty-eight modules or fourteen hours each week. Experience has shown this to be a workable distribution of teaching and preparation time. It has enough student-teacher contact to make it financially feasible and yet gives teachers adequate time for depth preparation.

Students doing research work during their independent study time often consulted with the Teacher Presenters and the Teacher Leaders. While this wasn't possible to calculate, owing to its variability, it had to be considered in scheduling released time for teachers. An attempt was made to have several teachers in each content field free each module of the day to help students who wanted assistance.

The Rejection of Staff Rank

The roles of the Teacher Presenter and the Teacher Leader were important to the instructional process at Lakeview. Spirited debate went on during the program's planning time as to whether the Teacher Presenter or the Teacher Leader was of prime importance. Good presentations were felt to be vital to the kind of motivation desired for the small groups, yet the importance of an effective small group teacher was obvious. After the Plan was in operation, it was universally recognized that neither role was more important than the other. Both were absolutely necessary if quality instruction were to result.

It was further agreed that the development of special talents for either role was the goal of the program and that no attempt should be made to encourage all teachers to seek one rank or position. Both good Teacher Presenters and Teacher Leaders were needed.

While the "master" teacher concept, whereby some staff members are designated as the best in the profession, has its appeal, it should be applicable to either role. Therefore, we hoped that some teachers would aspire and work to be "master" teachers in each role.

Finding teachers to lecture is a much easier job than locating teachers to work intimately with individuals and small groups. The quality of American education will increase as the teaching profession develops more specialists who work with students rather than talk to them.

An Extra Load

It needs to be pointed out forcefully that the Decatur-Lakeview Plan placed an additional load on each teacher. The decisions which were necessary to develop the program required uncounted hours of outside of class study and meeting time. It wasn't the procedures of this specific plan which caused the additional staff work; but any deviation from the norm requires extraordinary time consumption if it is to be thoughtfully executed. Lakeview teachers gave of themselves in an unusual way to examine their program, reshape its form and alter its substance.

The burden placed on the staff by the professional critics, who themselves were harnessed to the beaten path of instructional tradition, took its toll in the expenditure of both time and energy. This was unfortunate. It couldn't be avoided. Somehow the staff felt defensive about remarks made by other school people and went out of their way to answer questions and write articles for newspapers and journals.

Much time was consumed by the countless visitors to the Lakeview building. Of course, the visitors wanted to see how such a program operated and the staff usually gave of their time for explanations and discussions. The price for this innovation in education was paid in time lost from the entire staff's work week. The hope was, however, that the visitors would go back to their schools and improve on what they saw at Lakeview. The staff felt that entertaining the visitors was an obligation they owed to the profession. Sometimes visitors came for an hour and sometimes for two days. Often they forgot they were one of hundreds who visited each year and wanted to claim excessive amounts of time from almost everyone on the staff.

One teacher said, "The Decatur-Lakeview Plan didn't make teaching easier, but it did make it tasty and satisfying. We are teaching better now and enjoying it more."

The Loyal Opposition

Not all the staff bought all the aspects of the Decatur-Lakeview Plan. As a matter of fact, almost any piece of the Plan found some critics within the staff. However, the whole staff agreed on the total package and worked unceasingly to refine it when it was required.

The fundamental principles about how youngsters learn and the purposes of the large and small groups with independent study were agreed upon *in toto* by the teachers. Opinions differed on the way to put theory into practice. These were foundations on which decisions were ultimately made. Such divergence at the planning level was stimulating and healthy, for the progress made in the Plan's development came from decisions made as a result of these disagreements.

Frequently the advocates of a point changed their position, and vice versa, once the test of experience was made. An example of this was a heated controversy which raged among the staff on the point of whether or not bells were needed to identify the students who were tardy. The pros and cons were discussed. The heads of the departments made the decision to operate for a semester without bells. After the bells were dropped and punctuality increased, the critics were not only silenced but strong advocates of ruling tardy bells out of all schools!

From time to time a staff member would slip over from the practices of the Decatur-Lakeview Plan into the procedures of the Little Red Schoolhouse. Impatience with progress and frustration with change were dotted along the path. Each time they came back to the new design, though, after thought on their part or some bit of inspiration from another staff member. The response of the staff, when viewed as a whole, was thrilling.

The Selection of a Place for Change in Education

Often administrators and members of boards of education dream of the ideal school. Too frequently this fantasy begins with a clean slate of faculty members and, depending on who is doing the dreaming, of board members. Such is only a fantasy or a once-in-an-eighty-thousand opportunity. Improvement through change in education will occur for most of us only through a regeneration of the people already in the classrooms and in the policy bodies.

Constructive change in a school comes best in a situation in which the people are known to one another and in which the strengths and weaknesses are recognized and, it is hoped, understood. The first step in bringing about improvement in a school is to open a channel of communication through which ideas and sentiments can flow among all the people who make up the school. The point here is that change and improvement can take place in any school situation so long as the channel for problem identification is open and so long as there is leadership to set the atmosphere for testing ideas.

The Lakeview school staff had been in existence for twelve years when the Decatur-Lakeview Plan was first discussed. The staff already had entrenched alignments and established patterns of operation. These were considered worthwhile and laudatory. All was well. The change-agent was noticed when a challenge was given to these successful school practitioners to find an even better way for students to learn.

No attempt was made to transfer staff to other buildings in the system or find new jobs for some staff members in other districts. While opportunities were always available for teachers to go elsewhere, no teachers felt forced into leaving because of the Decatur-Lakeview Plan. The desire of the administrators was to change teaching practice, not to rid the school of any individual teachers. The thought was that the worth of the Plan would in part be judged as it applied to a somewhat typical staff. No special effort was made, then, to bring together a new faculty especially dedicated to the principles of the Plan.

The Decatur-Lakeview Plan was studied and formulated by all the staff. This is not to say that every teacher hammered out all pieces of the Decatur-Lakeview Plan. It is to say that some staff, in varying numbers and for different durations, worked on all the decisions and each of the procedures in the total package. It was implemented gradually. First one teacher tried one innovation, then another joined the first. Soon the total Plan was operative. As one teacher commented, "Old dogs can learn new tricks. It takes, though, another old dog to teach them."

As new people were selected for staff positions, an attempt was made to get people who would be supple in their thinking and would join in with staff. Converting tenure Lakeview staff was one matter, re-educating the new additions was quite another. We didn't mind having the loyal opposition among the tenure teachers, but we didn't want opposition from new teachers who weren't able readily to see the merits and procedures of the Plan. The big problem was the orientation of the new staff, especially those with previous teaching experience. The original staff went through the processes of the Plan's birth and early life. The staff additions didn't have this advantage. Though extra orientation sessions were held, these weren't as profitable for the new staff as the previous experiences of the seasoned faculty members.

The Advantages to the Teacher

The Decatur-Lakeview Plan had some definite advantages for the teachers. These weren't applicable to every staff member though they were generally true.

First, it gave most of the teachers a sense of pride in being a part of a bold attempt to do something to improve education. Lakeview teachers felt they were on the offensive in working toward the improvement of American public education. A missionary zeal developed for doing a job which really counted.

Second, the Plan brought teachers of the same content background together to test ideas and share approaches and techniques. Increased satisfaction with teaching was apparent through the adult associations developed by the team relationships. There is a particular kind of loneliness in a self-contained classroom, in spite of the presence of thirty youngsters. This disappeared in the team teaching situation.

Third, as teachers specialized in certain phases of the instructional process they generally received increased satisfaction. People like to do the things they are good at doing. As the teachers enjoyed their roles, they became more expert at teaching.

Fourth, the attitude of the students toward teachers was altered. Teachers became helpers, interested listeners and reliable sources of knowledge in the students' eyes. Teachers liked this. A new attitude appeared in the school which raised the status of both students and teachers in the estimation of one another.

Fifth, the independent study carried on by students was a source of pride and satisfaction to the staff. Independent study activities gave the staff a sense of being real teachers, in addition to purveyors of knowledge. Teachers saw the results of their teaching translated into student achievement.

The Needs of the Staff

A staff which is expected to make changes in a school must feel personally secure, but also must know that examination of ideas and

A COMPARISON OF THE TEACHING ROLE IN A TRADITIONAL SITUATION AND IN THE DECATUR-LAKEVIEW PLAN

Traditional Organization:

Teacher:

8:00	Money-Collecting, etc.
	Duplicating Materials
	Preparing Multimedia Aids
	Correcting Papers
	Hall, Ground and Study Supv.
	Individual Student Aid
	Record Keeping
	Evaluation
	Assignment Construction
	Student Experience Design
	Content Presentation
	Motivation
4:00	Professional Study

At the left are some of the tasks and and responsibilities each teacher performs to varying degrees almost every instructional day under the traditional organization for instruction.

Some of these functions require professional ability while others are less demanding in terms of specialized talent. At some of these functions some teachers are far superior than at others.

Decatur-Lakeview Organization:

At the right and below are divisions of kinds of teaching tasks into clusters of related functions giving a specialized responsibility for each staff member as employed in the Decatur-Lakeview Plan.

Teachers have fewer kinds of activities to perform, thus, it is assumed the teacher can do what he likes best, is best at doing. The specialization of function implies increased effectiveness. Non-certified personnel can do the non-professional duties and teachers can be reserved for teaching.

Teacher Presenter:

Evaluation	8:00
Assignment Construction	
Content Presentation	
Motivation	
Professional Study	4:00

Paraprofessional Worker:

Correcting Papers	8:00
Duplicating Materials	
Preparing Multimedia Aids	
Money-Collecting, etc.	
Hall Supervision	
Record Keeping	4:00

Teacher Leader:

8:00	Study Supervision
	Individual Aid
	Student Experience Design
4:00	Professional Study

practices is no reflection on the estimate of personalities. Without a firm sense of security, little innovation will take place in any school. Security here is not only related to job tenure, but it is tied in with a sense of belonging to a group, a feeling that each person is important and has something to contribute. Ample opportunity needs to be given staff members to express their hopes, ideas, fears and aspirations. Both a formal and informal structure needs to exist in a school if it is to satisfy the needs of the faculty members.

The Lakeview staff was told repeatedly, by word and deed, that failure of one practice was not a professional calamity. So a presentation by panel was not as good as planned. The important thing was that the motive was pure and effort was expended to do the best. What more could anyone ask?

The Lakeview administrators made a concerted effort to encourage teachers as they worked on the Plan. Sometimes it was in a personal conference; at other times it was in the casual remarks of a faculty meeting and at different times it was in the faculty weekly bulletins. Teachers need to be told when they are doing a good job.

Each administrative decision should be considered in the light of its influence on the staff. Once this basic consideration is understood by a faculty, the administrator will have little difficulty in doing whatever must be done. So long as their position is fairly considered, teachers tend to react favorably. Teachers, and rightly so, need to know what the administrators are doing and why they are doing it. Any wise innovator on the administrative level will keep this in mind.

No teacher should feel pushed into making a basic decision about how or what he will teach, but some need to be prodded into doing the things which are a consequence of basic decisions. For instance, once a teacher wants to work with a large group, he needs to be nudged into varying his pace in content presentation and encouraged to use visuals to put across the essential points of the presentation. Sometimes it's push, other times pull, and still other times it's wait!

Chapter
Fifteen

Non-Professionals Can Make
Teachers More Effective

THERE are countless functions the non-certified semi-skilled worker can perform to support the teaching process. It doesn't take a baccalaureate degree to prepare overhead projector transparencies, duplicate resource materials, correct objective tests, fill in required reports, do routine filing or scores of other supporting functions to the teaching process. Each of these tasks contributes significantly to the learning process. Their necessity is without question, but their importance is secondary to the operations the teacher performs. There is a place in the schools for personnel who specialize in doing these clerical and non-technical tasks. The professional teacher should be free to teach.

177

Problems in Seeing the Use of Assistants for Teachers

All of the chores which do not require a decision related to curriculum and which do not call for student contact can be performed as well by non-certified associates as by the teachers themselves. There has never been much use of non-certified workers in the public schools outside of the principal's office and, in some cases, the library. The precedent of not having these workers in other areas is difficult to overcome for two reasons. First, many teachers don't know how to use secretarial assistance. Somehow teachers seem to think the test isn't a valid test unless it is typed and duplicated by its creator. The imaginative use of assistants escapes others. For instance, a teacher working on a unit in history on the Period of Restoration could get valuable help in content design by asking the secretary to go to the Instructional Materials Center and bring back all the background material on this topic.

A second reason the precedent is difficult to overcome is that many boards of education have overlooked the benefits of this use of their resources. The fault for this must be put squarely on the shoulders of the school administrators. The employment of non-certified staff members need not be in addition to the employment of certified teachers, but may be in place of some. When functions are rearranged, class sizes varied and a critical look is taken at the use of teachers' time in a school, the budget often is ample for the substitution of non-certified for certified staff. In this age of teacher shortages the employment of non-certified personnel doesn't mean a teacher is displaced or discharged. It means that he is joined by a supporting subordinate worker in working with an increased number of students.

The Economics of Clerical Aides

As has been suggested, a school can reduce the number of teachers required through the reassignment of the routine duties to clerical aides. It is folly to say that the use of aides will or will not reduce total school operating costs. The total expenditure of funds of a school district is influenced by staff salaries, pupil-teacher ratio, capital outlay expenditures and the amount spent on instructional supplies. The motive of the policy-makers will determine whether money is to be saved through the use of paraprofessionals. Some schools who have used non-certified personnel claim they have saved money. Others have added technicians at increased cost. The single motive was to improve instruction.

Can you imagine the cost of going to visit a doctor if he didn't have a receptionist, a nurse and the help of medical technicians? What could a really creative architect build in a lifetime if he didn't have the draftsman and the field engineer to assist him? Educators need to examine seriously the possible profitable results of adding helpers to the instructional staff to free teachers to teach, to do the thing they are educated to do. What a waster of precious talent it is to misuse professional talent in doing routine clerical chores. However, these non-professional duties need to be done and will continue to consume teachers' time and keep them from students until the schools do what the medical and other professions have been doing for some time, delegating semi-skilled duties to non-technical personnel.

Purposes of Employing Non-Certified Aides

Lightening the teaching load is not a prime reason for considering the addition of teacher aides. Basically, the purpose is to make it possible for teachers to do those things with students that help improve the learning process. It elevates the job specification of the teacher to a higher plan by eliminating the clerical and non-technical operations teachers are asked to do. Teachers, then, are able to spend more time working with individual students.

These technicians can often do their jobs in a manner superior to the teaching staff. For instance, some clerical aides can type materials faster and much better than some teachers. The skill of typing is not always concurrent with the ability to teach, yet the skills of an efficient typist can benefit the teaching process.

Few teachers have the artistic ability to prepare dynamic visuals for use in instruction, let alone have the time to do it on a day-to-day basis. A person with this ability can be selected to specialize in serving the staff and do nothing but prepare bulletin boards that teach, mock-ups that explain and transparencies for use on the overhead projector that communicate in a very effective way. Once one does a job over and over he becomes proficient and quick at it.

The presence of adults in a school, whether certified or non-certified in itself has some spill-over advantages. Students can get an increased access to the certified staff when the paraprofessionals are doing the routine operations.

Specific or General Assignment

Once the decision is made as to whether or not paraprofessionals shall be used, the assignment of their time should be made and the job specifications set. The non-certified staff can be organized into a general pool to be used by all the staff as the need exists or the aides can be assigned to the various teaching teams or departments.

A visit to a school with the non-certified aides assigned to various departments revealed enthusiastic support of this plan on the part of the administrators and teachers. It was obvious though that the full advantages of the use of the paraprofessionals' time wasn't realized all the time. During certain peak work load times the clerks were swamped and during other periods there was a slack in their activity. Also, the science aide was more skillful in compiling bibliographies than the aide assigned to the social studies department. As a result, the particular skills of the aides were restricted to their department at the expense of other teachers.

The decision was made at Lakeview before the Decatur-Lakeview Plan was inaugurated to use all non-certified help through a pool. That is, work assignments were to be fed into a central location and to be done by the person with the time and ability to get the best results. The merit in this organization of clerks was that the paraprofessionals could specialize in the things they were good at doing.

An Approach to the Beginning

Owing to the relative lack of reference to the use of paraprofessionals in the literature and to our general inexperience, the Lakeview administrators employed the principle of gradualism in introducing the use of non-certified aides in the school. Full-time paraprofessionals were not employed on a salary basis.

Recognizing that volunteer groups of housewives are used to advantage in hospitals, welfare agencies and churches, the administrators approached the Decatur Junior Welfare Association and asked them to donate some time for doing supporting activities for the teachers. This group of public-spirited women accepted the call and gave of their time and energy. They were the experimental group who helped us decide how paraprofessionals could be used effectively in a school.

A general orientation session was held in which the purposes of the pilot program in the use of non-certified assistance were given. The volunteer workers were taken on a tour of the facilities and introduced to the staff with whom they would be working. To help establish a feeling of familiarity with the school, a special handbook was prepared for the volunteers. This gave a rundown on school policies and spelled out the operational procedures for the program.

The workers came to Lakeview on a schedule selected by them the first year. This was not, it turned out, the best arrangement since it was difficult for the assistant principal to keep the work coordinated. During the second year an attempt was made to develop regular work hours for each volunteer.

The ladies typed tests, corrected papers, worked out a grade analysis, catalogued books, created bulletin boards and did other such jobs. The central purpose of calling on these women was not to think of their organization as the permanent solution, but to verify the need for and test the influences of non-teaching personnel in the school. From this standpoint the project was a success. It was apparent, however, that volunteer assistance would be no substitute for the full-time employment of the paraprofessional.

Teachers gained from this experiment in that they began to see uses for the aides they had not formerly envisioned. A number of chores, filing and typing, which had been put off for a later day were done. Some of the staff found it difficult to give up their routine work to the aides without extreme caution, however.

The members of the Parent-Teachers Association Board also

rendered service, not as an organization activity, but as individuals. It was obvious that things were being done which weren't previously being completed at Lakeview because of the work of these aides. The additional help made it possible for teachers to increase their contact with students. The results of the routine filing, verifying and cataloguing of books in the Instructional Materials Center made the project worthwhile by itself.

An advantage resulted which was not intended by having the volunteer groups in the schools. An increased understanding resulted among the volunteers of the operation about the problems confronted in providing quality education for a diverse population. The volunteers appeared to give added support to the schools as a result of their new familiarity with the activities of a modern secondary school. There was real profit for both the citizenry and the schools in bringing people into a school on a regular basis when school was in session.

Full-time paraprofessionals paid by the board of education were not yet added to the staff, but the experiences of the volunteer aides proved the need for non-certified workers. The staff recommended their addition without hesitation as a result of the early experiences with the volunteer workers.

Classification of Aides

A classification system of the paraprofessionals was agreed on by the staff for use when they are added. Three categories of job descriptions were established. Each one would require different training and would receive special compensation. All of these workers would work a fifty-hour week and would be employed on the days school was in session.

PARAPROFESSIONAL ORGANIZATION		
Classification		
Instructional Aide	Responsible for correcting papers, doing assigned research, helping draft work sheets.	Bachelor's degree with specific content background

PARAPROFESSIONAL ORGANIZATION (continued)		
Clerk	Responsible for routine work: types, duplicates, prepares essential reports, takes attendance, makes visuals, etc.	High school graduation with secretarial skills
General Aide	Responsible for student supervision in cafeteria, halls, extra-curricular activities.	High school graduation, some college

While some authorities are advocating the use of non-certified personnel in the classrooms to follow teacher direction in the learning situation, this use was not a part of the thinking of the framers of the Decatur-Lakeview Plan. The paraprofessionals' role at Lakeview was intended to be non-technical in nature and restricted to performing processes which did not require student contact.

Chapter
Sixteen

Program Development Through
Professional Involvement

CHANGE is the rule of life! This law of nature unquestionably has application in education. Advances in both the content fields and in the psychology of learning are being made at such a terrific rate that an alert school can no longer rely on any degree-granting institute of higher learning to supply a teacher who will keep abreast of the times. The wonderful lines from *Alice in Wonderland* put today's problem in perspective: "You've got to run just to stand still."

A planned program of professional development was needed particularly by a school that was going to depart from the traditional pattern of instruction. Also, as the staff composition changed through additions, promotions and retirement, a retraining job was necessary. A school, as a social institution, must keep in tune with the current state of understandings. The best way to do this was through the continuous program of professional staff study. Somehow what was studied in a university summer school had little impact on teaching practice. Its emphasis was on theory without application. The staff study during a regular school year had the valuable advantage of making the principles under consideration more meaningful and realistic, for they were immediately tested in actual practice in a situation that counted.

Staff study during a year brought co-workers together and solidified their offense on an actual school problem. The Lakeview staff, for instance, got its programmed instruction in operation as the direct result of a group study. Nine teachers worked one evening each week for a semester with the assistant principal to decide how programmed instruction would benefit the curriculum. Some learning programs were purchased, others borrowed and still others were written by the staff. Trials were made with Lakeview students. Stimulation was given to the other staff members by those who experienced success in the development and use of the programs. Problems were mutually understood by a group who knew all of the circumstances. Both emotional and psychological help was given by the members of this study group to each other.

The Way to Keep Up

The public schools must be always responsive to the times. In an age of vast development of ideas and great accumulation of knowledge, the need becomes more pressing for a continuing study of the content fields.

In social studies it was most unfortunate to find the high school United States history class concentrating on colonial history to the exclusion of the social movements which have shaped our times. The in-service education program, then, for social studies teachers was to include a study of the capitalistic system as it has been translated into the democratic welfare state of today. The social studies teachers felt the need for a number of depth discussions of the curriculum.

In addition to content, in-service programs were concerned with methods of instruction. Like the content fields, significant studies have been afoot in the psychology of learning. Retention studies, for instance, have given us valuable clues to how facts need to be presented, using a multisensory approach in concept development, if effective learning is to take place. It was through in-service studies that such theory was eventually translated into practice.

Few school systems can always staff classrooms with teachers prepared in content and methodology for the courses needed by high school students. For instance, it is the rule today to find prospective teachers of English who have more preparation in literature than in grammar and composition. The lack of college preparation in composition and grammar must be compensated for in the in-service education program in the schools. While economic geography finds a place in many high school programs, few universities prepare social studies teachers adequately for this instructional responsibility. There is a need for in-service courses to bridge the gap between teacher-training programs in the universities and teacher assignments in the schools.

Learning More Concerning Learning

We no longer think of the educational process as being limited to cognition, but recognize that it is a process of interaction of facts, ideas, thoughts, feelings and behavior. Learning is not a matter of filling voids with data; it is the internal rearrangement of complex systems of perceptions, attitudes, feelings, skill, knowledge. This being true, a teacher is more than a store of related facts. He needs to be a highly skilled expert in stimulating personal growth and behavior change in diverse human population.

Staff members approached instructional problems in their own seminar sessions. Teachers who felt good about buzz sessions in their staff considerations had a model for use in their classroom practice.

The recognition of purpose was often more difficult than the means of achieving it. That is, noble motives were sometimes lost in faulty instructional practice. Also, when people—doctors, plumbers, lawyers, electricians, yes, teachers—are not given help in job growth, the urge of the individual to be content with the *status quo* is the result.

The task of the administrator was to inspire self-development of each staff member. Dissatisfaction with professional behavior must be shown in such a way that no reflection is made on the teacher as a person. The question asked over and over at Lakeview was: How can we do an even better job? The "even better" is an important sentiment to communicate. Teachers can add to their skill of instruction, as the Lakeview experience has shown, through intensive in-service experiences.

The Lakeview experience seemed to verify that summer workshops conducted by local boards of education for their own teachers will play a greater role in improving instructional practices and upgrading content within schools.

Educators somehow feel the urge "to discover America all over again" in setting up in-service programs by ignoring the accumulation of research already amassed on the characteristics of effective programs of in-service education. Before the Lakeview program was undertaken, the literature on the subject was reviewed.

Principles of a Professional Growth Plan

There were some guiding principles and practices accepted at Lakeview in formulating the in-service program.

Principle One: The program was based on the felt needs of the participants.

Until there was an awareness of an intellectual inadequacy on the part of the people to be in the program, there was little use in structuring even the best program. The administrator's first step, if the program was to begin from the top, was to create a feeling of need on the part of the staff. Some of the best programs for study came from the needs identified by staff members. Others came from the administrator's suggestions.

Principle Two: The participants had an important role in structuring the ground rules for the program; that is, those in the program agreed on the time of meeting, the length of sessions and the consultants, if some were to be used. The atmosphere for an in-service program was every bit as important as the atmosphere for any learning activity. The same ground rules needed to apply!

Principle Three: The participants were involved as much as possible in the activities of the program.

The best in-service programs were those which influenced tomorrow's instruction. For these activities to result in a change in behavior of teachers, the participants had to identify their practical concerns with those being studied.

Principle Four: Theory presented at such programs had to be applicable by the participants in their class work.

There was a demand for the participants to work out their application of the concepts suggested in each aspect of the professional development program.

There were multiple approaches to in-service education used. Each had a purpose and an application; a ranking order now would be impossible to construct.

It is a cardinal sin to force any staff member to participate in an in-service program. There are enough indirect pressures on a staff for such professional activity without direct insistence that teachers participate in any specific program. Readiness is a vital consideration for teachers in a professional development study.

Below is a list of the Lakeview avenues to in-service growth:

1. *Faculty Meetings*—with small group discussions of one or two ideas or problems of universal interest.

2. *Visitation Program*—whereby teachers visit other teachers or other schools.

3. *Workshops*—set up with a common goal or for a specific purpose paced by group progress on matters of common concern.

4. *Department Meetings*—with a single narrow topic for consideration with appropriate leadership and adequate resource information.

5. *Field Trips*—by staff to places of interest for application by the persons involved.

6. *Committees formed by special interest*—with a specific function and common causes.

7. *Independent Study*—as noted by personal need and individual or small group development.

8. *Formal Course Work*—offered by a visiting or extension professor.

9. *Conferences or Meetings*—at which people with common professional interests meet.

Perhaps one of the administrator's most important functions today is the organization of the in-service education program within his sphere of responsibility.

The Summer Workshop

The National Association of Secondary School Principals Commission on the Study of Staff Utilization in the Secondary Schools made two modest grants which enabled summer workshops to be held for two consecutive summers. During these sessions the participating staff considered the implications of small and large group instruction with independent study. Also, some part of each week was given to the specific course planning involving the ideas discussed in the general sessions.

The participants in the summer programs chose to participate in the workshops. The results were extremely beneficial. As a science teacher said, "We found time to do the kind of thinking, planning and gathering of resource material that we never had in a busy school year."

The decisions made in the summer staff workshops were presented to the faculty before school began in September. Some were shattered. However, enough were accepted and reinforced to make it possible to see change take place in teacher behavior in the large and small groups. Over and over references were made to the summer workshops during ensuing school years. The lack of instructional pressure in the summer, the large blocks of time for reading and research, and the lively discussion sessions made it possible for real progress to be made.

During one summer session students were brought in and teachers actually tried the techniques of instruction under consideration.

Many of these sessions were put on tape and these were played back for the entire workshop group. Lively discussions followed—especially on the question of the involvement of the teacher leader.

Other teachers prepared large group sessions and gave them to the workshop group for evaluation. This too was beneficial in showing the way for employing improved techniques of instruction. The staff was objective in hammering out effective procedures for employment of the techniques in question for the next year in the large groups.

A great deal of latitude was given in the use teachers could make of workshop time, but it was firmly established that the concerns had to be related to the common problems of large and small group instruction with independent study. Some teachers did a quantity of reading in the literature; others worked out specific procedures for their own use.

The principal and assistant principal served as workshop directors. The schedule was adjusted or modified as the group felt necessary. Interestingly enough, more time was spent on the techniques of small group discussion and independent study than on the program and techniques of large group work. The staff sensed the parts of the program in which it was most difficult to generate student interest. Outside consultants were used sparingly. These workshops were teacher-centered enterprises.

The literature was often consulted and ideas were shared as to how to get the theory into practice. For example, it was agreed that the pace of a thirty-minute lecture should be broken at least three times to call back wandering minds and to give mental relief from prolonged concentration on a point, but it took practice to get this to be the rule of instruction. Significantly, though, with many teachers it did get to be the mode of operation by the end of the summer workshop.

Visitation Programs

A series of visitations was set up for teachers who wanted to visit other schools noted for significant practices. The motive was to give teachers an opportunity to compare their performance with the practices of others. The faculty got a great deal from their visits. Staff trips were valuable in stimulating innovation.

An evaluation of the various in-service activities found the visitations high on the list. Lakeview teachers could easily identify what they were doing when they visited other teachers in schools with solid reputations. The schools selected for visits were those with programs similar to the one at Lakeview.

When a car was sent out at least four staff members went. The conversations which transpired on the ride to and from the other school were of advantage to the teachers and ultimately to the program. Most often, teachers would return to Lakeview with the opinion that Lakeview's program was superior to the program visited. This confidence was, in itself, worth the visit. Sometimes the teacher-to-teacher communication on the visits resulted in further professional contacts which added a new dimension to their teaching.

Another program of visitation was set up whereby teachers visited other teachers within the Lakeview building. This too had beneficial results. The innate competitive spirit of seeing "if I can do the job better than you" was called into play. Further, the teacher visited was given almost as many desirable benefits as the teachers making the visits.

Some preparation should be given teachers as to what to look for in making class visits. The worth of observing instruction is not always fully realized by the individual, regardless of how competent he may be in the actual teaching process.

Faculty Meetings

How often have faculty meetings been held which were administrative and not educational in nature? A faculty committee, the Professional Growth Committee, was concerned about the nature of faculty meetings. They felt those things which could be said by means of bulletin should be. Faculty meetings should be, they reasoned, decision-making or educational in nature. The Professional Growth Committee members worked on a program to make staff meetings worthwhile. Specific topics were suggested by the Professional Growth

Committee each month. Below are the topics they submitted for one year:

September—The Assignment: Busy Work or Productive Instructional Experience

October   —Potentials and Possibilities of Programmed Instruction

November—Individual Differences in Learning and Understanding

December—Multimedia Approaches to Instruction

January   —Examinations: A Tool to Teaching and Evaluating

February   —The Slow Learner Is Still a Learner

March   —Open for Discussion With the Guidance Staff

April   —Promising Practices in Small Group Instruction

May   —Recommendations for Program Improvement for the Next Year

One or two staff members made presentations based on experiences or the literature at a few meetings. Discussion sessions followed. Sometimes the faculty divided into buzz groups. Recorders kept track of group agreement and strong sentiments. These were compiled and fed back to the staff within a few days after the meeting. Out of these buzz groups grew understanding on current issues and, at the same time, solid recommendations for further study.

If there were a fault with Lakeview faculty meetings it was the fact that administrators took too much time in making announcements and mentioning trivia. Frequently, outstanding instructional jobs done by staff members were reported to the total staff by the principal. This did two things. It gave recognition to those deserving it and it projected a model for others to emulate.

A staff which doesn't meet cannot act in concert. Staff meetings require, if they are to be worthwhile, time to structure and prepare. The dividends are multiple. The value in having everyone hear the same theory and the advantage of all being present for a discussion period is without parallel for program development.

It is telling to note that the meetings teachers voted as superior were those in which there was a high degree of staff participation. Those rated the lowest were those consumed with lengthy presentations from outsiders. Lakeview teachers preferred to work on their problems and to hear from their own group members.

Department Meetings

The department meeting was the clearinghouse of ideas. Each month there were at least two department meetings, though others were called as the need existed. The topics considered were related to specific concerns of teachers of one content field. Text selection, recommendations for materials for the Instructional Materials Center, grouping specifications and other such matters were of central concern to the departments.

An attempt was made to establish in department meetings an atmosphere in which any idea was worthy of presentation and in which teacher recommendations on ways to improve the Decatur-Lakeview Plan were sought. These, in turn, were submitted to the principal for approval before implementation.

The in-service aspect of the department meeting came in the planned program of consideration of assigned topics. Each department was given resource materials for the topic of the month, often in the form of a position paper. Teachers studied these, reacted to them and either agreed or made alterations. Both the principal and the department heads worked out the department study topics.

A list of one department's topics will illustrate:

SOCIAL STUDIES

September—What are the Places of Fact Presentation and Concept Discussion in the Social Studies?

October　—What are the Desired Outcomes of Social Studies Instruction?

November—Where Can the Instructional Materials Center Help the Social Studies Teacher?

December—What is the Place of the Judeo-Christian Tradition in High School Social Studies?

January　—Who Should Present Lectures in the Social Studies?

February —What are Worthwhile Independent Study Projects for the Social Studies?

March   —How Can Anthropology Be Introduced at Lakeview?

April   —What Recordings Are Appropriate and Available for Use in the Social Studies?

May   —What Are the Needs for the Staff for the Next Year in Terms of Program Development?

The department heads served as small group leaders with the central responsibility going to the staff for discussion. These small group meetings of people unified by a general content interest encouraged inquiry into the particular subject field. Reports of conventions, readings, and visits also were made in these meetings. The department head served as the educational leader in his department for his content area.

Interest Committees

As interest in a subject developed, because of a concern with a present practice or because of new developments, special faculty committees were formed on an *ad hoc* basis. Most often these committees cut across subject-matter lines. Some departments set up their own problem areas and pursued them together.

One group, for example, worked on identifying meaningful small group techniques. Some far-reaching changes were evidenced in the way teachers performed in the small groups. These are only a few of the many groups which were organized, worked on problems and then disbanded. Their work lived on after them.

The Decatur-Lakeview Plan Was In-Service Education

The Decatur-Lakeview Plan can be rightfully considered a gigantic in-service education program. Staff members tried to seek solutions to old problems by giving emphasis to the theories developed on improved ways for youngsters to learn.

The thought behind much work with staff was that before youngsters' learning behavior is to change in a marked fashion, teachers' instructional behavior needs to change. The Lakeview staff was involved to varying degrees in the many phases of the in-service program. If anything, once the pace was set, the job was to slow staff members down and encourage them to avoid over-extending their time and energy. The intellectual curiosity which leads people into teaching also makes a dynamic in-service program accepted and enjoyed by the staff.

The building administrator becomes the teachers' teacher. By challenging, by inspiring, by providing materials, by giving opportunity "to do," he leads the staff in the in-service program. Without this intensive in-service program there would not have been a Decatur-Lakeview Plan.

To some staff members the many professional development activities were interesting and valuable experiences; to others they were only mildly appreciated and enjoyed. What appealed to one staff member was sour milk to another. The success of the in-service program was its diversity and its policy of permissive participation.

The Building Approach

At Lakeview an approach was made to developing administrative understanding of new trends in the content fields, and to concentrating on instructional matters by viewing administration as a team effort. The line authority network was a paper structure. In reality the principal and the three other administrators met twice a week— or more often—to share ideas. The only time the role of one member of the team became pronounced was in the ultimate decision stage, for which the principal assumed full responsibility.

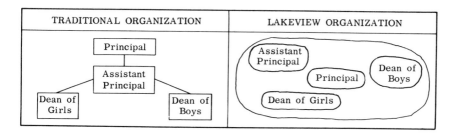

The same principles of specialized area of function, restriction of ranges of operation and cooperative planning that went on with the teaching teams went on with the administrative team. After the formal day was over or in a lull in the midmorning, the administrative team met to talk about the strengths and weaknesses of the small groups, the potentials for increased use of multimedia aids or schedule potentials to make learning easier and better.

A Firm Stand and Diverse Vistas

We felt a firm stand was needed on those elements of the instructional process which were shaped into the Decatur-Lakeview Plan. Once we agreed that we would structure a program of small and large groups with independent study, we stood up to be counted. The idea was not to be a breastbeater or a noisy advocate of a point of view, but to make certain what we believed in was communicated.

At no time did we say more than is in this account, but we did put ourselves on the side of the Trump Proposals as they were modified for the Decatur-Lakeview situation. We answered questions asked, regardless of their sting or consequence, based on this approach to instruction.

We read as much as time would allow, everything from programmed textbooks to doctoral dissertations secured from a neighboring university center. Members of the administration contributed their findings from observation, reading or discussion to other members of the team in our bi-weekly sessions. This helped solidify beliefs about the system of instruction we were advocating and kept us all in touch with the advances in the field of secondary education.

Chapter
Seventeen

A Lay Advisory Committee
and the Decatur-Lakeview Plan

SOMEHOW the whole can be greater than all its parts when speaking of a lay advisory committee. A group of solid thinkers with a broad school interest can bring community attitudes and general public impressions to the school and, in return, can interpret the school staff's goals and operational procedures to the citizenry.

The lay advisory committee is a mirror of the community which reflects general sentiments about most aspects of the school's operation. Certainly no lay committee can become a policy-making body, but it can become a policy and administrative evaluation group. At the same time, the lay advisory committee members are in a position to know the facts and be able to discuss them over the community's coffee cups and back hedges.

The lay committee keeps the school close to the parental public. A building principal can duplicate the advisory role a board of education serves with the lay committee on the building or neighborhood level. Decatur has over twenty-two thousand students trooping to thirty-six schools each day. The superintendent and the board of education can easily be disassociated from the stream of one segment of the town's thought. The lay committee is the school's compass which directs the development of individual program character and personality. It is a foolish dream to visualize one school like all others, particularly in a large community. Differences in socio-economic status, educational experience and aspiration, school size and staff competence cause variations in any district-wide curriculum. The lay committee helps the building administrators and school staff tailor-make the district policies to fit the particular school's requirements.

Functions of the Lay Committee

The Lakeview Lay Advisory Committee served two constructive purposes in the development of the Decatur-Lakeview Plan. First, this group gave the administrators a good idea of both the school's image in the community and of any expressed parental concerns about any aspects of the Plan. Second, the committee members were ambassadors without portfolio to each of the neighborhoods in the school's territory.

Before the decision was made to establish the advisory group, the staff members agreed that this was not to be a group of straw men; rather, the lay committee was to be composed of the strongest leaders and the best thinkers in the school area. The administrators decided at the outset that they would listen carefully to what the group said, regardless of its point of view. The tendency of too many educators is to form advisory committees to give widespread credibility to a predetermined idea. The Lakeview group was set up to be a genuine advisory committee. Respect was to be given to the membership's opinions. School board members may have an eye to the next election; lay advisory committee members are only concerned with what is best for the next generation.

The avowed purpose of the committee was to organize a group of parents who could function as consultants on the Decatur-Lakeview Plan. The group became much more. The advice they gave, sometimes quite indirectly, about bus routes, grading procedures, disciplinary problems and about the attitude of the community was very helpful to the staff. While the committee seldom had much to offer on what the school should do, it was helpful in giving valuable advice on how the Plan's objectives could be met. The school ship was not steered by the lay committee, but the speed and path the administration took was influenced by the thinking of the committee.

At the outset we decided that we didn't want the Lakeview program to be far different from what the community believed of it. Without widespread understanding the Plan could neither be inaugurated successfully nor endure for any length of time. The Plan has been successfully inaugurated; time will test its strength.

Lay Advisory Committee Membership

The Lakeview Lay Advisory Committee had fifty-four members. There was an even distribution of parents from each of the six grade levels. In sending out the invitations an attempt was made to include residents from all parts of the school's area. When fifty-four letters of invitation went out we assumed only one-half or maybe two-thirds would return a positive reply for membership. Such was not the case. A one hundred per cent positive reaction resulted. The four building administrators and six representatives from the faculty joined the committee to complete its membership.

Each principal knows where the school's loyal supporters are. The active school friends are to be found in the Parent Teachers Association Board of Directors, the Booster Club and in other school groups. The fact that those people are already banded together means they are involved in the school program. Although every school needs and depends on these actively engaged people, different types of people need to be included in a lay committee. The Lakeview Lay Advisory Committee was not to be more of the same. The school's critics, its apathetic observers and enthusiastic friends all needed to be on the lay committee. It was intended to be composed of a representative sample of the community population. A few who worked hard for the school were included with those who were usually strangers to the school, except perhaps at Christmas programs or graduation. The criterion for membership was not how responsive the potential members would be to the school's past performance, but how accurately the members would reflect the parental viewpoint about the instructional program at Lakeview.

Some members invited to membership were known to be the most vocal critics of the school and its program. We thought that if a skeptic could be converted to the cause, the program would be more readily accepted by the less hostile people of the community. Then, too, there was the thought that, like a converted sinner, there is no one as militant as an adversary turned ally.

This selective procedure got the administrators into some hot water. Some parents looked on this committee as an honor for esteemed community leaders and were miffed at not being included. Others bothered were the long-time school workers who felt they weren't adequately appreciated because they weren't included. Of course, such wasn't true. You couldn't get a cross section of the community by including only the highly interested and diligent workers.

The Lakeview Area

The Lakeview area is typical of many school areas in that there is a high community interest in educational matters. There has been a tradition of interest in curriculum and a community pride in the school that makes it quite natural for almost everyone to talk about the school and how it is operated. As is the case in educational matters, some people in the area feel they know, because of their educational experience, as much or more about the operation of a modern instructional program than the professional staff. In spite of this basal feeling, all were agreeable to hearing out a presentation of the facts about the Plan.

While there are some deviations, of course, from group norms, the residents of the Lakeview area are sincerely interested in education for their children and expect to be active in making decisions about their school. One cannot help, when working in the area, but develop a feeling of affection for the Lakeview area residents. The strong loyalties that prevail in the area soon encircle the school staff.

There is a broad range of representatives of all the socio-economic, cultural and interest groups in the area. The school is the single force that unifies the people from diverse vocational and social interests. Many people in the area attend churches in other parts of the Decatur community. Few people work in the geographic bounds of this residential school district. Factory workers, service personnel, merchants and a scattering of professional people comprise the Lakeview community. The lay committee was a microcosm community.

The residents of the area are generally people of principle. They are militant in their convictions on almost any issue. The school district is not all in the corporate limits of the City of Decatur. A battle rages on in public meetings, the news media and even in the courts as to whether annexation of the Lakeview area to the city is proper. The Lakeview school is already included in the Decatur School District. A significant point in showing the character of the people is that on school matters the proponents and opponents of the annexation issue joined together in common discussion and came to general agreement on questions and answers concerned with education. The leaders of both factions in the city annexation issue served on the Lay Advisory Committee.

The residents of the area were a pleasure for the school staff to work with. Heated discussion and wide breaches in point of view on the details might exist, but the big issues of the youngsters' welfare and worth of education were never questioned. When the need was shown, the voters in the district marched to the polls and put tax increase on increase to finance the kind of schools they wanted.

Such a community presents a paradox, for it is both easy and difficult for the staff to work in the Lakeview area. In educational goals there is no problem. On paying for a quality program there has not been a negative attitude; but the number of individual contacts with parents is gigantic compared to neighboring schools. Lakeview parents are a part of their children's lives to the maximum extent that their children allow and are, therefore, willing and sometimes even anxious to talk to Miss Jones about a wrong answer on a test paper. Lakeview parents do not assume the "school is always right" attitude. They want to know all the facts on almost every issue before the adult judgment is formulated.

Unfortunately, a block of parents was never reached by the school, either through regular group programs or by individual contacts. The guidance staff and administrators dealt most often with those who needed the least help, while a sizable group wasn't touched by the school. The Parent Teachers Association couldn't muster interest or participation from a segment of the school population. The lay advisory committee was intended as a means to bridge this gap.

The committee formed to study the Decatur-Lakeview Plan was not the first experience the parents had with lay committees in the Lakeview School. Over the years a number had been formed. The last one was organized three years earlier to consider an accelerated program for students of above-average achievement. The idea was to form a committee for a special study purpose, keep it in operation for as long as there was both interest and a need and then disband it. No attempt was made to prolong the life of an organization that had lost its purpose. While some membership was carried over from one committee to another, the members were new, for the most part, each time an advisory committee came into existence.

Meetings of the Lay Committee

In the beginning the administrators thought the lay committee would probably meet once each month or six weeks. How wrong this was. At the first meeting the group decided that meetings would be held every other week. Later, they were held every third week. While most school groups adjourned for the summer, the Lakeview Lay Advisory Committee didn't. Meetings went on regardless of the toll taken by vacations and other necessities.

A chairman, a vice-chairman and a secretary were elected by the committee. The chairman presided over the meetings and set the tone of each meeting. The agenda was suggested for the first meeting by the principal and thereafter it was determined by the committee with the counsel of the principal.

The agenda was sent to the members in advance of each meeting.

This gave ample opportunity for personal thought and neighborhood discussions. Also, the minutes of each session were duplicated and mailed. Other enclosures were mailed in these letters giving data requested by the group. These matters ranged from per-pupil cost to teaching load to abstracts from the research on retention studies. Homework, in the form of background material, was sent out to the membership before the meeting.

Over the months a formula for the meetings emerged. Usually the committee would meet, hear a presentation, break into small discussion groups to consider the elements of the presentation and then report back to the large group. The focus of the activities of the lay group was on how the parents in the community felt about the new program, the building changes, the implications for staff and so forth. The discussion sections of five to seven members were rewarding to the committee's purpose and satisfying to the committee members. Once decisions were reached in the small groups, reports were made to the committee as a whole. Here it was fascinating to see the points of agreement on the Decatur-Lakeview Plan develop.

A freewheeling atmosphere prevailed at these meetings. Few ideas were sacred and the discussions were candid and penetrating. The parents were interested in what was going to happen in the large groups. They had a concern about the possible confusion which could result from a lack of agreement and coordination between the various members of the teaching team. The desire for evaluation from semester to semester was expressed. Parents wanted to know the nature and amount of content students were learning in the new plan as contrasted with the traditional program. The membership soon became intensively involved in the problems of the Plan, as well as with general educational concerns.

By-products of the Lay Advisory Meetings

It wasn't long before most members of the lay advisory committee looked on the Decatur-Lakeview Plan as their property. They took to the stump to explain it to neighbors and friends. In countless informal ways the subject of the Decatur-Lakeview Plan invaded the community. Always the anticipation of discussions on education quickened among non-school groups when lay committee members were present. These people knew the facts and were anxious to talk about them.

Some pride was developed in the point of view that Lakeview was a school answering the critics of education with a planned program for improvement. It was not long before the lay advisory members were well versed in both the theory and application procedures of the Decatur-Lakeview Plan. No longer were glittering generalities about "improvements in program," "refinements in procedure" and other nebulous phrases the fortress for the school's advocates. Instead they were armed with an understanding of how pupils learn, of the ways the school was organized to facilitate understanding and of the manner in which both financial and human resources were used.

Lay Committee Takes an Active Role

The cause of education was served best when the community knew its problems and understood its projected solutions. The lay committee recognized this and decided that a formal community education program was necessary. The members of the committee agreed to set up a speakers' bureau. The Decatur-Lakeview Plan was explained to service clubs in the larger Decatur community, to the listeners and viewers of both radio and television and to parent groups in all of the grade schools sending pupils to Lakeview. These explanations were handled by the lay committee. Sometimes a teacher went with the panel or sometimes a single speaker did the job. The people of the community liked to hear about the new program from their fellow citizens. Educational jargon was eliminated from the content of the speeches and the enthusiasm of the parents was a thrilling experience for listeners. The administrators welcomed the lay committees' assumption of this responsibility because it took a public relations burden off the administrators and gave them more time for the program.

The lay committee wasn't satisfied with verbal communication to explain the Plan to the Lakeview residents. They wanted to put out a booklet which told the story of the Plan's origin and gave the rationale for its operation. This was written by the assistant principal and revised countless times by a subcommittee of the large advisory group. It employed a generous use of pictures and a few diagrams to give the message. This was sent, after universal agreement was reached, to all the parents in the area.

The stage was set by the Lakeview Lay Advisory Committee for the Plan to go into operation at the appointed date. If there was a danger, it was that too much was expected of an instructional program in too brief a time span. Caution was given over and over about expecting learning behavior to change overnight. Pleas were made to look for improvement in steps and not to expect leaps. Indications were that the people generally understood and liked the elements included in the Decatur-Lakeview Plan.

The Real Contribution

The most worthwhile contribution that the lay committee made was not in the area of public interpretation of the program, important and beneficial as this was. The real contribution to the Plan's development was the penetrating questions asked about teaching and learning. The rigor of the questions and the isolation of important issues about the large and small groups was invaluable to the administrators. The lay committee members were skeptical enough to cause the proposals to get unusual scrutiny by the professional staff. True, the staff studied each principle implied in the Plan's proposal, but the lay committee raised countless questions concerning operation which were valuable to the full-scale implementation of the large and small groups.

There is nothing wrong with defending what we do in the schools on a specific point-by-point basis. It is a good exercise in judgment and tends to validate or refute staff decisions. On some issues the staff decisions were not fully accepted, even after prolonged discussion; but the staff knew where the professional judgment and lay opinion differed. For instance, the lay committee was concerned about the assignment of long-range projects. They felt students profited more from daily work accounting than from a single project consuming several weeks' effort. The staff held to the view that the advantage of long-range planning and independent work in a content area was more beneficial. The long-term projects were adopted. The parents, although they didn't agree, understood the staff view and accepted it.

The suggestions which came out of this group's considerations were multiple. For example, it was recommended that a visitation schedule be set up for the parents to come to school during the day to observe school in operation, to hear the large groups, to see the small groups and to watch students in independent study. The Parent Teachers Association took this on as a project and carried it out. After the tours, coffee sessions were held during which an administrator came in and answered questions and talked about the school's goals. Another suggestion was related to the need for more facilities. The lay committee members wanted the addition of facilities that administrators felt timid in seeking.

The Lakeview Lay Advisory Committee was set up to consider the proposals in the Decatur-Lakeview Plan. When the Plan was in operation for a year, the purpose of the committee was achieved, and the group dissolved. Perhaps further advisory aid will be required in the future. When the circumstances make another committee necessary, such should be called into action.

Once a citizen is a member of such a group, the attitudes developed linger on for years. It has not been an uncommon situation for a Lakeview administrator to meet a person far removed from current school affairs who fondly recalls participation in a previous lay committee activity.

It was interesting to note that some of the lay committee members understood more about the program than the professional staff in other buildings in the system and most of the members of the central office staff. The participants read all the materials sent to them and discussed the ideas and procedures in the group meetings.

The lay advisory committee helps give meaning instead of lip service to the belief that the schools belong to the people. The lay advisory committee helps people feel the ownership and brings out the best kind of protective feelings which result in school improvement and serve as an advantage to the school's total instructional program.

Chapter
Eighteen

Problems of Implementation

ANY account of a demonstration project in education would be woefully inadequate if mention were not made of the problems inherent in making adjustments in a school, a dynamic social institution. Certainly there were problems in getting the Decatur-Lakeview Plan in operation. There were, also, problems when the school was organized in the traditional way. Problems of finance, personnel barbs, parental frustration and student difficulties were neither dissolved nor created by the existence of the Decatur-Lakeview Plan.

Walter Bagehot, the nineteenth century philosopher, once said, "One of the greatest pains to human nature is the pain of a new idea." This thought was applicable to the Decatur-Lakeview Plan in the minds of some. Few disagreed with the logic or the conclusions in the proposal. Each idea seemed

207

to make sense when isolated and evaluated. The problem came, however, when the label, Decatur-Lakeview Plan, was assigned to the project and when it was viewed in its entirety. Somehow people felt minor changes were all right for schools to make, but sweeping alterations were disturbing.

Concerns About the Decatur-Lakeview Plan

Never did we hear anyone, whether erudite educator or caustic critic, argue that the Plan was apt to harm the students or that its motives were less than lofty. We did hear outcries that it was new and different. Those who were concerned about the Decatur-Lakeview Plan were bothered that such a change should take place in Decatur without ever having taken place before, even though the rationale of the Plan was accepted by them in its entirety. The references given which told them of the various elements of the Plan operative in other individual schools fell on deaf ears. There was some resistance to the idea of wholesale innovation, regardless of precedence. This did not discourage the staff; the skeptics were, by and large, ax-grinders with a biased view.

Some members of the American Federation of Teachers group, for example, were critical of the varying teacher loads in the Plan. They were completely opposed to the thought of employing non-certified people to work with the teachers. This group envisioned a day when salaries may be different for various members of the school staff. These unionists were fearful that fewer teachers would be used than in a traditional organization.

Another group of skeptics were the watchdogs of the public purse who looked on the project as a potentially more expensive instructional program. How the Plan influenced quality of instruction was less important to this group than its possible cost.

All the objectors were given frank answers to their questions. Often these rebuttals sharpened the differences between the Lakeview staff and some of the concerned people, but others were won over to the staff's point of view.

The Other Edge of the Sword

The people in the Lakeview community generally were avid supporters of the project. When the board of education considered altering the boundaries and thus causing some students to have to go to a neighboring school in the same school district, a hue and cry went up. The representative of the parents in the area said at the board meeting, "We want our youngsters in the Lakeview School. We like the program there and feel it is right for our children."

If there was a problem with the people in the Lakeview district, it was that they were overzealous in praising the program and making claims the staff couldn't support. While it was a fact that the percentage of the graduates doubled within a four-year period, the Plan was not totally responsible. Some of the good things which happened would have occurred without the Decatur-Lakeview Plan. Maintaining an attitude of objectivity when a successful program is operated is difficult for any school's community.

Lakeview visitors to other schools reported some horrible instruction in several affluent and highly regarded school communities. This is often glossed over because the products, the students of these institutions, do well, but not as well as they could and should, in college and in competitive examinations. People generally want to like their school and sometimes go to extremes to find reasons to justify their pride.

Of course, the staff was pleased when parental appreciation was shown for both the idea and the application of the Plan. This frequently stimulated greater efforts for the innovation's success among the staff members.

The Problems Within the Profession

By far the largest number of bricks hurled at the staff for developing the Decatur-Lakeview Plan came from the teachers in other Decatur secondary schools. The reasons for the criticism were not defined. A shadow of doubt was cast on the sanity and competency of a staff who would be a part of such a large-scale school improvement program by some teachers in other buildings within the system. The administrators in the other schools were effective in defending the Plan whenever they could. Some representative of the Lakeview staff spoke to six of the other seven secondary school staffs during the second year of the Plan's operation to answer questions. In each case the speaker was well received and treated with unusual courtesy. Still reports would come in about reckless statements being made by teachers in other buildings.

One story making the rounds was that Lakeview teachers required faculty meetings after dinner several times a week to hold the program together. Other equally ridiculous tales left the impression the Plan was a "teacher killer" and the staff members were totally exhausted. Although it was true Lakeview teachers put forth added effort, it was wrong to draw the implications that some did. Perhaps such tales were a result of natural narration growth as it makes the rounds. Deep resentment of these rumors developed in some Lakeview staff members, who knew how smoothly the operation was going.

At the same time, the teachers and educators who visited Lakeview were filled with praise and expressed real satisfaction with what they saw. The strongest advocates outside the staff and community were the professionals from other school districts. We kept a file of these letters of testimony and were pleased to note the good number who went home and adopted some phases of the Decatur-Lakeview Plan.

Perhaps a visitation system should have been set up within the Decatur Schools to allow teachers from the other buildings to visit the Lakeview building when it was in operation.

The Visitation Drain

During one school year we kept track of the number of visitors who came to spend a day or two to see the school in operation. The number who signed in was well over four hundred. In addition, there were untold numbers who dropped in unannounced. The visitors came from near and far. New York sent administrators. Teachers came from Iowa and Ohio. Arkansas was represented by both teachers and administrators. California visitors wanted to see how a school breaks tradition and moves into an individualized instructional program. This became a drain on all the Lakeview staff concerned.

Although we were glad to see visitors, the teaching tasks required a full day and the hospitality routine sometimes became taxing. Of course, each person who came had questions and comments. Unfortunately, we didn't have anyone on the staff who could concentrate on guiding tours and explaining the program. Some people were met and shown around by the principal; others were taken about by other staff members. We tried to keep the visitors satisfied, but this couldn't always be done. The requirements of Lakeview students came first. When a visitor made a request which had a possibility of interfering with learning, it was unceremoniously denied.

We didn't change a thing for any visitor. Business always went on as usual. The students paid little attention to the procession. They were, regardless of the occasion, as the song in *Annie Get Your Gun* says, "doin' what comes naturally."

There is great value for all schools in sending out visitation teams. We recognized this and we did it. The problem comes though in the tremendous numbers which alight in any one place. After the first year, during the first two months of school we just didn't allow any visitors. We wanted the setting to be stable before visitors came in droves. This caused some miffed feelings but we felt this policy was in the students' best interests. A gentleman who came from Oregon without any notification was more than mildly upset when he didn't get to make a class visitation.

Various schemes were attempted to handle the visitation traffic. We thought we could handle them in groups. This didn't work. Plane and travel schedules interfered. We assigned students who were able and willing to take the visitors around the school and answer questions. This too failed. The traveling administrators and teachers wanted to see and talk with teachers and administrators. We assembled written descriptions of the Plan. Always questions arose not covered in the material. One of the strong motives for this book was to give a complete description of the Plan to the profession.

Administrators' Problems

The Lakeview administrators assumed a heavy load in the implementation of the Plan. This took a toll on outside interests and cut sharply into family life. More safeguards should have been made against this. The job became a passion. The goal of getting the program fully refined and perfectly operative in every detail was noble, but the pace set in going at it was excessive.

Handling routine matters, working with the in-service program, writing staff bulletins, finding background information and working with teachers and students is a full-time job. Schools which are committed to real program improvement need to commit resources for securing competent people to get the job done. While the Lakeview administrative team never flinched before any time demands, it would have been better for both the program and for the administration if some matters of secondary importance had gone undone.

The Lakeview administrators spent too much time away from their school and their program as the Plan developed. Speaking engagements and professional organizational demands created a pressure. While these requests made the administrators feel somewhat exhilarated, they took away from the leadership role in the building. As one teacher said, "I had to go to a state meeting to hear about how the principal thinks we are doing."

Central office administrators could help pilot the program's progress if professional obligations were reduced. The circle, of course, is endless. People who have demonstrated they can do things are sought to do others. A balance was needed between local school needs, system requirements for time and professional organizational participation. Certainly all were important so long as the order of importance was maintained.

Schools who want to be substantially better should provide adequate administrative help.

Faculty Problems

As a staff implements a new instructional procedure, some restraint from evaluation should be made for the period of time between their desire to change and the time at which the alteration is an accomplished fact. Too often there is a feeling that a desire is in itself the accomplished product. Teachers and programs cannot be evaluated on their motives alone. Time needs to be extended to make it possible for the intention to become a reality.

The faculty, both as a group and individually, needed to be given a lot of reassurance as they changed their instructional behavior. Without a doubt, the major task of the administrators was to develop a sense of operational security within the staff.

One day a visiting dean of a school of education casually observed to a Lakeview small group teacher that she wasn't really worth a full pay check for the day. His comment was based on his observation of a student-centered class in which this teacher made only three suggestions to the group in the entire hour meeting of the class. When the dean left the teacher expressed her concern at her respected visitor's remark. The teacher really was doing a terrific job. While the number of interjections was only three, the quality was high. This teacher needed reassurance that teachers often serve students best by letting the learners talk, express and verify.

Not one teacher left Lakeview because of the Decatur-Lakeview Plan. Some found more lucrative and responsible educational assignments. These were as a direct result of their participation in a school's effort which was doing things. Problems of implementation did not arise on the faculty level. The staff took to their plan like the proverbial ducks do to water.

It would have been helpful if a conference could have been arranged for teachers from other team teaching schools. The association and exchange of ideas and concerns with others in similar roles were very helpful. This contention was validated by the National Science Foundation's Biological Science Curriculum Study's procedure of setting up demonstration centers. There were five or six schools in a close geographic area selected to try these new materials. The teachers from each of these schools met to do their planning and evaluating. The Lakeview science department participated in this program in its early stages. The procedure of bringing teachers of similar interests together encouraged valuable emulation.

Miscellaneous funds acquired on the building level from speeches, consultant assignments and articles were used to get the faculty the extras they felt they needed. A rich supply of books was acquired on the topics of theory and practice of small groups. These reference works were used extensively by some of the staff. Others felt the need for materials not provided by the board of education catalog of instructional supplies. When a staff member felt an absolute requirement for these, they were added. It is amazing what the purchase of a few extra items did, for example, to get the mock-ups in use!

As any staff member tried one of the new approaches, he needed to get another's opinion of its worth. The independent study assignments were of real concern to some teachers. As they geared work to high or low ability students there was some concern as to whether or not something was too complex or too rudimentary. Assurances had to be given that deviations from the norm were valuable. Emphasis had to be placed on the worth of the assignment for the learner. Here again it was necessary to support the fact that teachers were right when they extended theory into application.

Student Problems

There was a pronounced absence of student problems in implementing the Decatur-Lakeview Plan.

It was infrequent that students used the shelter of newness to excuse their own lack of application to scholastic matters. By and large, the students did very well. Implementation problems came from outside of school organization, not from within. The letters in form of testimony which came from graduates—some in the service, some in college and some working—made the effort worthwhile.

Community Problems

Another pointed fact was that there were no problems within the Lakeview community with the establishment of the Decatur-Lakeview Plan. Perhaps this was due to the extensive coverage given the innovation by the local press. The Lakeview Lay Advisory Committee was also responsible for this pleasant circumstance.

Good instructional procedures were readily recognized and easily accepted. Appendix III gives the question-and-answer information the parents were given by the Lay Committee.

Educators Can Do Something About It

A disciplined sense of competition must be instilled in school people to encourage the search for improved ways to teach. Too often school people pit their school's worth against another's by salary schedules, co-curricular offerings and pupil-teacher ratios. The important concern isn't what we have, but how to develop and utilize what is at hand.

Too often, decisions about what a school will do in terms of periods in the day, methods of instruction and so forth are determined by the results of a survey about what others currently are doing. It is almost as if ignorance were surveying ignorance. We need more bright new schemes and promising proposals to consider.

Perhaps national professional conventions should set up programs in which theories that haven't been tried can be discussed. Somehow we must begin looking up and forward, not down or to the past. The day is over when educators should be concerned only with minor alterations and insignificant refinements in their school's organization. School leaders must seek dramatically better programs.

Some assignment of guilt, too, must be made to the professors of education who commit the original sin in the thought patterns of administrators. A study of the literature of educational administration reveals that change in education is generally considered to be adjustment and refinement rather than fundamental change. Some educational administration has been thought of as holding to the level of the prevailing practice. A "play it safe" attitude is often reflected by professors of education as they tell their students to beware of the straw men of community displeasure and/or general misunderstanding. Too much time is spent in graduate study on problems of cafeteria operation and public relations. It frequently looks like colleges of education are little more than storehouses of insignificant tradition.

Although the sensational influence of modern technology has, through modern communication, permeated society, education has not adopted the possibilities of technological advantage for instruction. Scarcity of funds is usually given as the reason for this lag, though scant attention is given to wholesale redeployment of school resources.

We cannot foresee the specific problems of the next generation but we can prepare free men to think for themselves and know how to unite for resolute action. School experiences need to be framed with this outcome in mind. The stimulation which one learner gets from another, the practice in contributing to the group, the preparation for the world of working with others after school are all important considerations for the educational administrator.

The Educational Administrator

The educational administrator has a role which has to date been poorly defined. This may be due to the relative youthfulness of administration as a profession. In the simple schools of a less complex age the administrator's role was related to the service and supervisory function. A generation ago the educational administrator kept store. Sometimes he hired staff; often a board member did this. The administrator purchased supplies, handled extreme discipline cases and handed out diplomas.

Today the school administrator is the instructional leader of his school(s). He needs to be abreast of the content fields and their developments, be a master of personnel management and, most important, create a climate for inquiry. The time has come for administrators to regard their role as one supported by what research has to say as well as what practical applications of theory can be made to reveal. He must bring out the teachers' talents and establish an atmosphere conducive to learning.

The administrative educator must establish recognized bounds of responsibility and authority if he is to be a positive force for progress in improving education in a community. The board of education-administrator relationship needs to be defined and then, the difficult part, respected. Who employs a lawyer and then dictates how he shall write the contract or sees a physician and rejects the diagnosis in favor of personal opinion? Effective educational administration is a profession which requires allegiance to the practitioner's judgment.

American public education needs more martyrs to the cause of holding the line against policy-makers and unknowing citizens who try and often succeed at dictating to the professional administrators. If one community cannot buy the ideas of the school administrator, then the beliefs should not be sacrificed just so one can keep sitting in the administrator's chair.

Things are out of tune when the members of a board of education have to suggest approaches to instructional problems. There must be enthusiasm on the part of the administrator for the new solutions to old problems. Administrators need to keep up with the research and advances in their field as do science teachers, medical doctors and engineers. When the demands are so great that this cannot be done, it is time to delegate duties or to add supporting personnel.

Chapter
Nineteen

Where Do We Go From Here?

TO talk about small and large group instruction in our secondary schools might well be to talk about achieving the goals of quality and universality in American education. Since World War II the big task of the schools has been to provide for the numbers of students—the vast quantity of needed teachers, buildings, supplies and materials.

Times are changing. A public and a profession once glued to tradition are elevating their sights. More is wanted than quantity. Quality is the goal.

In an age when one-third of the nation's youth drop out of school before high school graduation, something must be done in our schools. Study after study documents the need for the schools to gear instruction to a different mental and psychological level for various students if the problem of wasted talent is to be solved. Perhaps varying class sizes will aid in this problem. Perhaps the sense of belonging, the pride in achieving, the self-realization through contributing in a small group class will make students who are prone to leave school early want to graduate. Certainly we need dynamic new teaching methods to solve the dropout problem.

The gigantic task of providing qualified teachers for the schools of the future can defy our comprehension.

The time has come for us to re-evaluate our use of precious teaching talent. We must seek ways to give as many students as possible contact with the best of the teaching profession.

We must pull our heads out of the sand and recognize there are functions of the teaching process which can be performed for the professional teacher by a non-certified aide. Thus, teaching talent can be reserved for contact with students. More students can be handled by fewer teachers when the non-certified personnel become a part of the teaching team.

In Content

The future will surely find public school educators giving more attention to content, the "what" of instruction. Large national attacks will continue to be made on problems of subject-matter selection for youngsters at various maturation levels. Local school districts, too, will be more concerned in the future about being narrow in learning experience selection and, at the same time, being broad in including the humanities and fine arts in the curriculum. The National Education Association's Center for Instruction, the National Science Foundation's several studies in curricular re-examination, the modern mathematics programs begun at the University of Illinois and carried on elsewhere, the United States Office of Education sponsorship of Project English and others are signs of the times. Careful study of what we teach youngsters is the order of the day.

Local school districts will begin to put more resources in curriculum development activities. Communities will want their teachers to have an effective program for teaching grammar and composition, as well as social studies, science and mathematics. To get the job done teachers will spend more time on curriculum development— both during the school year and during the non-school months. Research and scholarship specialists will continue to grow in number as members of school staffs.

While it isn't reasonable to reduce the professional education requirements for teaching, it is justifiable to increase the teaching area stipulations. Teachers will begin to concentrate on their teaching field to a greater degree than ever before as we spend more time talking and thinking about subject matter in content areas. That is, as schools become larger—and they surely will—the teacher will not be required to work in several fields, but will be restricted to one or perhaps two courses for instruction. As always happens with specialization, depth and breadth study will result.

New content areas will become a part of the educational diet of tomorrow's learners. Courses in anthropology, celestial science, and psychology are a few of the newer subjects all the students will investigate. To get all of these subjects in the curriculum some displacements will be made in what we now teach.

The Promise of the Future

Two changes will surely take place. First, we'll lengthen the school year and, in many communities, lengthen the school day. School will begin around 8:00 A.M. and extend to 4:00 P.M. Students will get more professional assistance in learning in tomorrow's schools. At the same time they will be free and encouraged more to work on their own.

The Instructional Materials Center will be staffed in such a way that students can use this storehouse of materials for the school in the evenings and on Saturdays. Hot-rod interests will shift to scholastic pursuits as the nation concentrates on the maximum development of the greatest resource of the universe, the human mind.

Second, we will re-evaluate what we teach and where we teach it. Foreign language, for example, will be found more commonly in the lower grades than is customary today. Elementary schools, for instance, will begin earlier teaching place geography. In grades seven and eight we will put emphasis on human geography. As we refine the curriculum, we will avoid some of the senseless repetition and foolish inclusions of content in the school program we have today. There will be an even flow of subject matter from the first year in school until the last. Public education will include the thirteenth and fourteenth years of instruction.

Ungraded Schools

The quality schools we will shape will be ungraded. That is, students will move through the instructional process at their own rate, irrespective of their grade or year in school. We will begin to look at youngsters in a more realistic light. When they are able to take up a new problem area, they will do so. The grade level notion of classifying students by years on earth surely will disappear. We will free the student to go to his capacity in each subject he studies.

Some students will move at a faster rate in some content areas than others. If a student can do higher mathematics in the eighth year in school, then he will be permitted, even encouraged to master it. If a tenth-year student has reached a reading level plateau, then he will stay with materials at this level, but study in breadth reading and communication skills.

The measure of what a student does in school will be made by his transcript of courses taken and achievement standards met, not by a high school diploma per se. Schools will be expected to teach students to think, to discriminate, to judge, to recognize and to act according to the individual's measure of ability.

The ungraded school of the future will have realistic expectations for learners. The student who is unable to comprehend a subject discipline will be channeled into instructional experiences appropriate for his talent and self-realization. We are on the verge of using practices to individualize instruction. Perhaps the Melbourne High School in Melbourne, Florida, and its dynamic principal, B. Frank Brown, are blazing a trail others will follow.*

The ungraded school is a common-sense approach to providing for differences between and within people. Some youngsters are able

* See B. Frank Brown, *The Nongraded High School* (Englewood Cliffs, N. J.: Prentice-Hall, Inc., 1963).

at mathematics and poor in social science, or vice versa. The school of the future will identify differences of ability in children and make provisions for them.

This report is of a school which has not yet become ungraded, but is approaching it by means of altered instructional practice, through different organizational procedures. The Decatur-Lakeview Plan is a step toward the ungraded, student-centered school.

The New Emphasis

In the schools of the next quarter century students will be freer to learn. The school will be organized so students can work independently. Learning laboratories for both academic and non-academic areas will replace the egg crate buildings we have today. Harold Gores, President of Educational Facilities Laboratory, once remarked, "Today we aren't as far away from the one-room schoolhouse as we imagine. Instead of the single rooms being scattered over twenty miles, we've hooked them all together under one roof."

The new emphasis will be putting responsibility for learning on the students. Teachers will spend more time listening to what students know and don't know. Then, after gauging the student's state of understanding, the teacher will make appropriate learning prescriptions to get at increased knowledge.

The time students spend in school will be distributed in a different fashion. Sometimes students will be with teachers, sometimes alone in study carrels with a rich supply of written materials. Audio stores will be at hand for youngsters to listen to explanations on logical processes and literary works on tapes and disks. Learning programs will be at hand to help students learn facts and understand principles so teachers can be more valuable in helping students see relationships and go into studies in depth.

Students of all socio-economic backgrounds will be the realistic concern of the schools. A breakthrough in keeping all students in school longer will come when more guidance counselors are a part of the school staff. When the school's ungraded program allows culturally disadvantaged youngsters to be a part of a special program geared to their previous experiences and unique needs, a major hurdle will have been cleared.

Boards of Education

The concept of local control of education is rapidly changing. Although the schools of a half-century ago were controlled almost exclusively on a local level, the schools of the future will be assisted by more state and federal money, requirements and advisory counseling.

The Constitution gives the power for education to the states. In turn the states have delegated the operational aspects to local boards of education. As is always true in our democratic society, when one level of government doesn't adequately fulfill an obligation or perform a service, another level steps in to give assistance.

Those who oppose more involvement in educational affairs on the part of the state and the federal government would do well to give added support to the local board of education. A vote against a bond issue or a referendum is a vote for more federal aid to schools.

If the various states don't contribute more to education to finance the kind of instructional program our society needs, we can be dead sure we'll have additional federal aid and regulation of schools. The choice is ours: Either support the local board to a greater extent or relinquish control to the state. If the states don't satisfy the requirements for education of a modern technological society, then the federal government must attempt to do the job.

Local control of schools, even with the growing amount of outside activity on the part of other governmental levels, is vital to quality instruction for each district. The balance of program needed in each school must be determined by the local board. If one school in a district needs more guidance services than another, then the local board can provide them. If the community is predominantly a college-oriented area, then the school can work to this end. Schools, like people, are different. Boards of education would do well to remember this and make compensating policies for the various schools in the district they operate.

The control local boards have is a tremendous potential for real improvement in the schools of the land. First, personnel selection is of primary importance to the local board. The lack of educational leadership which exists in some communities is the glaring fault of the board of education. The chief school officer in each district is the executive officer of the policy-makers. Also, he is the instructional leader of the staff. He should be accountable for the quality of the educational program. If he doesn't function adequately, then the board of education isn't fulfilling its role if he continues to stay in his position.

School boards of the future will be less concerned with the day-to-day operation of the school and will concentrate more on policy development. The thin line between administration and policy formation will need to be underscored if we are to get our horizons lifted.

Research and Demonstration

The field of educational research will continue to clear the underbrush of school practices. Each school will want to know more and more about its student population. The researchers will become a vital part of school district decision-making. On the local level the researchers will be charged with translating the findings of the ivory tower philosophers and theoreticians into instructional practice. Effective practice, rather than personal hunch, will be the deciding factor in both content and methodology.

The major contribution that the foundations and federal government can make to superior school practice is in the area of research. We need to know much more about the teaching process. When and how should we present each idea and every subject? The textbook publishers will take a back seat to the curriculum researchers in determining what our students will read and learn.

It will not be long until demonstration schools are scattered across the land. These schools will serve as lighthouses for others. Instead of reading or hearing of the significantly better way to teach, teachers and citizens will be able to visit and observe, first hand, how the practice is operative.

The spectacular development of agriculture in the United States has been stimulated by the demonstration plan. When a new hybrid is found, it is planted and the farmers in the area can see it grow. The ones who plant it can answer questions and explain how it was done. The nation needs demonstration schools where people can go to see how new curricula or new organizational patterns actually operate.

Teachers of the future will travel more in the pursuit of ideas about content and technique. The world, literally, will be the classroom. The wonders of the educational television operated within a building, and even in a classroom, aren't far in the offing. A video tape can record a lesson in science or an event in history in such a fashion that it is at the teacher's call by means of a flip of a switch. Technology, which has benefited modern man in business, industry and entertainment, cannot be shut out of the school much longer.

The Professional Staff

The professional staff of the future will also change. In addition to increased specialization in content, the methods of instruction must certainly improve. Although colleges appear to be holding to the professional training requirements of the past now, a new day must come. The intern concept used in the medical field will get added consideration by teacher preparatory institutions. The day may come when teachers serve as interns for a year's time before their professional study is completed. Teacher-training schools will concentrate more on the psychology of learning and give less emphasis to the history of American public education. The noteworthy chapters in this study are only beginning to be written.

As educational requirements for teachers increase, the academic quality of the profession will correspondingly improve. Teaching cannot help but attract inventive, creative minds who crave the intellectual excitement of this new age of the knowledge explosion. Increased salaries will contribute to general interest in teaching as a career.

The single salary schedule is going to be under careful scrutiny. While merit pay plans have been attacked as impossible to operate, they have been successful in some places for a long time. In Barrington, Illinois, for example, a merit plan has been in operation for decades. Teachers are compensated for their initiative, production, work with students and instructional effectiveness, not only by their years of experience. Teachers find their security in Barrington with their talents and not with their tenure.

Teachers will specialize in some parts of the teaching-learning process. Some will work with content and large groups. Others will work with small groups. Still others will not have class assignments as such but will be consumed with working with individuals in independent study.

The Role of Administration

Sometimes it seems that people regard education like the weather; everybody talks about it but no one does much to improve it. True, we build more buildings, hire more teachers and spend more money for housekeeping and bookkeeping, but the form and substance goes on without major alterations. Too few policy makers and educators are creative visionaries in search of drastic revisions of the schools aimed at effecting lasting improvements.

There are countless excuses for all concerned with education to worship at the altar of the *status quo*. The tides of enrollment that hit schools each year, the pressures on educators to defend and justify their practices and the placement of added social welfare responsibilities on public education dissipate energies that should be seeking better instructional organization.

Too much is expected of many educators. Keeping the ship sailing is a full-time job comprised of routine committee meetings, conferences with board members, and most of all, administrating one of the community's largest business enterprises. Educators need time to read, to discuss and, most important, to think.

Advances made in the content fields are occurring at a whirlwind pace. Somehow educational administration must keep abreast of progress; it must reshape the organization for instruction to facilitate the application of advances in all the content fields. Educational administration is a service profession to students and teachers. The school administrator is the broker between ideas and people. He must bring both together with a bond that will result in profit to the enterprise. The administrator is basically a leader who brings out the best in the professionals with whom he works and coordinates a balanced instructional program. He directs the program to suit the particular school and community needs.

The Spotlight

All of the changes and adjustments made in the schools will be to individualize instruction for students. The spotlight will be on the individual and how he can be assisted in reaching his full potential as a free man with limitless potential for self-realization.

The schools of the future will avoid gang teaching, group procedures and universal requirements. Each student will be encouraged and given the opportunity to seek the eternal truths in light of modern applications.

The Area of Change

The atmosphere of the school, the specifications for learning groups, the allocation of precious time and talent are the administrator's concern. The best means to achieve quality education is to individualize instruction. This means we teach students one by one, even when in groups, with their variance in interest, achievement, ability and personality characteristics. The trend toward teaching all students the same things has been reversed as the lower ability levels stay in school longer. As we learn more about gifted learners and we see the urgency for freeing the capacity of the individual for learning, for creating and for adapting, it is obvious changes in school organization are necessary.

The system of equal time for all subjects, regardless of complexity or learner's requirement for mastery, needs to be changed. We must have a school program which compensates for the different rate and level at which a student learns. The system of organization of large and small groups with independent study offers such potential. It does imply that teachers will teach in a new way since it requires that the instructor view each student as unique.

Although it is new today, in a quarter of a century only the lagging schools will be organized under the equal time system. Surely change in the form of instruction will continue as we develop clearer insights into curriculum construction and as we adjust the schools to the ever-changing form of society. Perhaps the day will come when all schools will be ungraded, when youngsters will progress through learning experiences without artificial interruptions brought about by grade and arbitrary content lines. Until this day comes, however, we need a program for learning to help us move from the practices of the past toward the needs of the future.

The following lines from Dickens' *A Tale of Two Cities* have application for American public education in our time:

> It was the best of times, it was the worst of times, it was the age of wisdom, it was the age of foolishness, it was the epoch of belief, it was the epoch of incredulity, it was the season of Light, it was the season of Darkness, it was the spring of hope, it was the winter of despair, we had everything before us, we had nothing before us, we were all going direct to Heaven, we were all going direct the other way—in short, the period was so far like the present period, that some of its noisiest authorities insisted on its being received, for good or for evil, in the superlative degree of comparison only.

Appendices

Appendix I

Comparison Table of Organization

A comparison table of organization and enrollment for the school as it would be organized in a traditional manner and as it is organized with the Decatur-Lakeview Plan.

The business of determining student elections and establishing staff needs is always difficult. Added complication resulted when a school was organized in a fashion that deviated from the norm as in the Decatur-Lakeview Plan. Therefore, the organizational pattern was figured in two ways, according to the traditional pattern (see Part One) and according to the Decatur-Lakeview Plan (see Part Two). Comparisons were made about staff needs and class sizes.

When the Decatur-Lakeview Plan was first proposed there were 758 students at Lakeview. After the second year of the operation there were 1,040 students enrolled. Adding to the complexity was the fact that we reduced the staff size by five in a school district-wide economy measure. These events, coupled with enrollment increase, have added to the teacher load in the areas of mathematics, science, English and social studies. This, we think, was one example of how the earlier reduction in staff influenced the instructional program. Yet, the utilization of staff in the Decatur-Lakeview Plan kept ratios on a more favorable level than the traditional organization would have provided.

On the other hand, the increase in school enrollment has tended to balance and create an efficient class size in art, business education, foreign languages, music and upper-division courses in science (physics and chemistry) and in mathematics (trigonometry and college algebra). Foreign language grew out of the pattern projected in our predictions, especially Latin and French. The others have held to the expected levels. Lakeview students take more subjects than they did prior to the Decatur-Lakeview Plan. Then only twenty-six per cent of the freshmen took five or more subjects and now seventy-five per cent take five subjects.

We felt that the recommendations for the use of professional staff time in Part Two were gratifying and promising in the better utilization of teacher talent and time. As we have more experience with large-small group instruction, we see the replacement of some professional positions for paraprofessional jobs.

The summary which follows compares traditional class organization with the organization of the Decatur-Lakeview Plan.

TENTATIVE ENROLLMENT

Enrollment Estimates:

	Boys	Girls	Total
7th Grade	96	94	190
8th Grade	93	104	197
9th Grade	101	95	196
10th Grade	96	93	189
11th Grade	76	72	148
12th Grade	70	50	120
			1040

PART I . . . ORGANIZATION TABLE FOR A TRADITIONAL SCHEDULE

Courses	Number of Students	Number of Sections	Average
Art Department			
7th Grade Art	190	6	31.6
8th Grade Art	187	6	31.1
Art Activities	33	1	33
Drawing and Painting	20	1	20
Applied Design	16	1	16
3-D Painting			
Business Education Department			
Basic Business	54	2	27
Typing 1, 2	89	3	29.6
Bookkeeping	40	2	20
Stenography	28	1	28
Sales and Law	24	1	24
Typing 3	19	1	(comb. with trans.)
Office Practice	27	1	27
Transcription	10	1	(comb. with typ. 3)
Office Occupations	15	1	15
Distributive Education	9	1	9
Driver Education Department			
Driver Training	92	3	5 (Blk. of time)
Driver Education	184	1	4 (Grps.)(1 day wk.)

(This number discounted those we expected to schedule for summer driver training.)

Courses	Number of Students	Number of Sections	Average
English Department			
7th Grade English	190	6	31.6
8th Grade English	187	6	31.1
English 1, 2	196	7	28
English 3, 4	184	6	30.6
English 5, 6	148	5	29.6
English 7, 8	60	2	30
English Honors	20	1	20
Business Communications	21	1	21
Practical English	19	1	19
Speech 1, 2	26	1	26
Speech and Drama	17	1	17
Echo	24	1	24
Dorian	28	1	28

Courses	Number of Students	Number of Sections	Average
Foreign Language Department			
Spanish 1, 2	39	2	19.5
Spanish 3, 5 (combined)	19	1	19
Spanish 7, 8	8	1	8
Russian 1, 2	31	1	31
French 1, 2	52	2	26
French 3, 4	27	1	27
French 5, 6	16	1	16
French 7, 8	11	1	11
Latin 1, 2	56	2	28
Latin 3, 4	34	1	34
Latin 5, 6	19	1	19
Latin 7, 8	14	1	14
Guidance Department			
7th Grade	190	In Homeroom	
8th Grade		In Homeroom	
9th Grade		6	32.6
Homemaking Department			
7th Grade Homemaking	94	5	18.8
8th Grade Homemaking	104	5	20.8
Homemaking 1, 2	38	2	19
Clothing	36	2	18
Foods	28	2	14
Family Living	21	1	21
Home Care of the Sick	17	1	17
Industrial Arts Department			
7th Grade Ind. Arts	96	5	19.2
8th Grade Ind. Arts	83	5	16.6
Industrial Arts 1, 2 *	59	3	19.3
Auto Mechanics *	46	2	23
Cabinet Making	19	1	19
Electricity	23	1	23
Drafting	28	1	28
Arch. Drafting *	17	1	17
Diversified Occupations *	16	1	16

* Experience indicated these courses would increase in enrollment by the opening of school.

Courses	Number of Students	Number of Sections	Average
Mathematics Department			
7th Grade Math	190	6	31.6
8th Grade Math	187	6	31.1
General Math	79	2	39.5
Algebra 1, 2	131	5	26.2
Plane Geometry	119	4	29.7
Algebra 3—Solid Geometry	51	2	25.5
Trig.—C. Alg.	39	1	39
Econ. Math (Gen. Math 3)	33	1	33
Music Department			
7th Grade Music	190	6	31.6
8th Grade Music	187	6	31.1
7th Grade Boys	26	1	26
7th Grade Girls	53	1	53
7th Grade Mixed	61	1	61
8th Grade Boys	17	1	17
8th Grade Girls	48	1	48
8th Grade Mixed	57	1	57
Cadet Band "A"	61	1	61
Cadet Band "B"	29	1	29
Choir (H.S. Frosh-Soph)	48	1	48
Choir (H.S. Jr-Sr)	27	1	27
Orchestra	8	1	8
Band Groups (H.S.)	93	2	46.5
Physical Education Department			
7th, G.P.E.	94	3	31.3
8th, G.P.E.	104	3	34.6
G.P.E., 1, 2	95	3	31.6
G.P.E., 3, 4	93	3	31
G.P.E., 5, 6	72	2	36
G.P.E., 7, 8	50 *	1	50
7th, B.P.E.	96	3	32
8th, B.P.E.	83	2	41.5
B.P.E., 1, 2	101	3	33.6
B.P.E., 3, 4	91	3	30.3
B.P.E., 5, 6	76	2	38
B.P.E., 7, 8	70 *	1	70

* Number would be dropped by approximately 9 due to vocational scheduling.

Courses	Number of Students	Number of Sections	Average
Health, 7th Grade			
Health, 8th Grade *			

* Other health classes—grades 9-12—were figured in with the regular classes.

Science Department

7th Grade Science	190	6	31.6
8th Grade Science	187	6	31.1
Physical Science 1, 2	84	3	28
Biology 1, 2	137	5	27.4
Adv. Biology	21	1	21
Chemistry	53	2	26.5
Physics	39	2	19.5
Air Science	20	1	20

Social Studies Department

7th Grade Social Studies	190	6	31.6
8th Grade Social Studies	187	6	31.1
Economic Geography	196	7	28
World History	184	6	30.6
U.S. History	148	5	29.6
Social & Govt. Problems	52	2	26
Student Council	33	1	33

Study Hall Supervision

Assuming the study area would hold an hourly capacity of 82 students and assuming a study room holds 40 students, we would need the following per teacher hours per week:

7th Grade	10
8th Grade	10
9th Grade	13
10th Grade	12
11th Grade	8
12th Grade	8

(These are distributed among the various departments and are minimum requirements.)

PART TWO . . . ORGANIZATION TABLE FOR DECATUR-LAKEVIEW PLAN SCHEDULE

Courses	Number of Students	Number of Sections	Average
Art Department			
7th Grade Art *	190	9	21
8th Grade Art *	187	9	20.8
Art Activities	33	1	33
Drawing & Painting	20	1 ⎫	36
Applied Design	16	1 ⎬	

* I day a week or 2 days a week for one semester.

Business Education Department			
Basic Business (L) *	54	1	54
Basic Business (S) **	54	4	13.5
Typing 1, 2	89	3	29.7
Bookkeeping (L)	40	1	40
Bookkeeping (S)	40	3	13.3
Stenography	28	1	28
Sales and Law	24	1	24
Typing 3	19	1	19
Office Practice	27	1	27
Transcription	10	1	10
Office Occupations	15	1	15
Distributive Education	9	1	9

* L—indicates Large Group class.
** S—indicates Small Group class.

Driver Education Department			
Driver Education (L)	184	1	184
Driver Education (S)	184	6	30.7
Driver Training	92	0	00
English Department			
7th Grade English (L)	163	1	163
7th Grade English (S)	163	10	16.3
7th Grade English I.H.	54	2	27
8th Grade English Honors	30	1	30
8th Grade English (L)	110	1	110
8th Grade English (S)	110	10	11
8th Grade English I.H.	47	2	23.5

Courses	Number of Students	Number of Sections	Average
English 1, 2 Honors	29	1	29
English 1, 2 (L)	119	1	119
English 1, 2 (S)	119	10	11.9
English 1, 2 I.H.	48	2	24
English 3, 4 Honors	29	1	29
English 3, 4 (L)	127	1	127
English 3, 4 (S)	127	10	12.7
English 3, 4 I.H.	28	1	28
English 5, 6 Honors	25	1	25
English 5, 6 (L)	96	1	96
English 5, 6 (S)	96	6	16
English 5, 6 I.H.	27	1	27
English 7, 8 Honors	20	1	20
English 7, 8 (L)	60	1	60
English 7, 8 (S)	60	5	12
Practical English	19	1	19
Business Communications (L)	21	1	21
Business Communications (S)	21	2	10.5
Speech 1, 2	26	1	26
Speech and Drama	17	1	17
Echo	24	1	24
Dorian	28	1	28

Foreign Language Department

Courses	Number of Students	Number of Sections	Average
Spanish 1, 2 (L)	39	1	39
Spanish 1, 2 (S)	39	2	19.5
Spanish 3, 4	19	1	19
Spanish 5, 6	8	1	8
Russian 1, 2	31	1	31
French 1, 2 (L)	52	1	52
French 1, 2 (S)	52	4	13
French 3, 4 (L)	41	1	41
French 3, 4 (S)	41	3	13.7
French 5, 6	16	1	16
French 7, 8	11	1	11
Latin 1, 2 (L)	56	1	56
Latin 1, 2 (S)	56	3	18.7
Latin 3, 4 (L)	34	1	34
Latin 3, 4 (S)	34	3	11.3
Latin 5, 6	19	1	19
Latin 7, 8	14	1	14

Courses	Number of Students	Number of Sections	Average
Guidance Department			
7th Grade Guidance	190	1	190
8th Grade Guidance	187	1	187
9th Grade Guidance	196	1	196
Homemaking Department			
7th Grade Homemaking (L)	94	1	94
7th Grade Homemaking (S)	94	8	11.75
8th Grade Homemaking (L)	104	1	104
8th Grade Homemaking (S)	104	10	10.4
Homemaking 1, 2	38	3	12.7
Foods 1, 2	28	2	14
Clothing 1, 2	36	2	18
Family Living	21	1	21
Home Care of the Sick	17	1	17
Industrial Arts Department			
7th Grade Ind. Arts (L)	96	1	96
7th Grade Ind. Arts (S)	96	8	12
8th Grade Ind. Arts (L)	83	1	83
8th Grade Ind. Arts (S)	83	8	10.4
Industrial Arts 1, 2	59	3	19.7
Auto Mechanics	46	2	23
Cabinet Making	19	1	19
Electricity	23	1	23
Drafting	28	1	28
Arch. Drafting	17	1	17
Mathematics Department			
7th Grade Math	190	6	31.7
8th Grade Math	150	5	30
8th Grade Algebra	37	1	37
General Math 1, 2 (L)	79	1	79
General Math 1, 2 (S)	79	8	9.9
Algebra 1, 2 (L)	131	1	131
Algebra 1, 2 (S)	131	9	14.5
Plane Geometry (L)	119	1	119
Plane Geometry (S)	119	9	13.2
Algebra 3—Solid Geom.	51	2	25.5
Trigonometry—Col. Alg.	39	1	39
Econ. Math (Gen. Math 3)	33	1	33

Courses	Number of Students	Number of Sections	Average
Music Department			
7th Grade Music	190	6	31.6
8th Grade Music	187	6	31.1
7th Grade Boys	26	1	26
7th Grade Girls	53	1	53
8th Grade Boys	61	1	61
8th Grade Girls	17	1	17
7th Grade Mixed	48	1	48
8th Grade Mixed	57	1	57
Cadet Band "A"	61	1	61
Cadet Band "B"	29	1	29
Choir (H.S.—Frosh-Soph)	48	1	48
Choir (H.S.—Jr-Sr)	27	1	27
Orchestra	8	1	8
Band Groups	93	2	46.5
Physical Education Department			
7th, G.P.E.	94	3	31.3
8th, G.P.E.	104	3	34.7
G.P.E., 1, 2	95	3	31.7
G.P.E., 3, 4	93	3	31
G.P.E., 5, 6	72	2	36
G.P.E., 7, 8	50	1	50
7th, B.P.E.	96	3	32
8th, B.P.E.	83	1	83
B.P.E., 1, 2	101	3	33.7
B.P.E., 3, 4	91	3	30.3
B.P.E., 5, 6	76	2	38
B.P.E., 7, 8	70	1	70
7th Grade Health (L)	190	1	190
8th Grade Health (L)	187	1	187
9th Grade Health (L)	196	1	196
10th Grade Health (L)	184	1	184
10th Grade Health (S)	184	10	18.4
11th Grade Health (L)	148	1	148
12th Grade Health	120	4	30
Science Department			
7th Grade Science	190	6	31.7
8th Grade Science (L)	160	1	160
8th Grade Science (S)	160	10	16

Courses	Number of Students	Number of Sections	Average
8th Grade Science I.H.	27	1	27
Physical Science 1, 2 (L)	60	1	60
Physical Science 1, 2 (S)	60	6	10
Biology 1, 2 (L)	137	1	137
Biology 1, 2 (S)	137	10	13.7
Advanced Biology	21	1	21
Chemistry (L)	64	1	64
Chemistry (S)	64	6	10.7
Physics (L)	39	1	39
Physics (S)	39	2	19.5
Air Science	20	1	20
Social Studies Department			
7th Grade Social Studies	190	6	31.7
8th Grade Social Studies (L)	160	1	160
8th Grade Social Studies (S)	160	12	13.3
8th Grade Soc. St. I.H.	27	1	27
Economic Geography 1, 2 (L)	150	1	150
Economic Geography 1, 2 (S)	150	10	15
Economic Geography 1, 2 I.H.	46	2	23
World History (L)	184	1	184
World History (S)	184	14	13.1
U.S. History (L)	148	10	14.8
Social & Govt. Problems	52	2	26

Based on the above, the following is the comparison of the staff organizational need according to a traditional schedule and according to the Decatur-Lakeview Plan.

Department:	Number of Teachers Needed	
	Traditional Schedule	Decatur-Lakeview Schedule
Art		
Teachers:	1	1

(This means the teacher would have classes of 38 in the junior high and 5 preparations with no time for department duties.)

Business Education		
Teachers:	4	3 1/2

Department:	Number of Teachers Needed	
	Traditional Schedule	Decatur-Lakeview Schedule
Driver Education Teachers:	4/5	3/5
English Teachers:	9	7 3/5
Foreign Language Teachers:	3 1/5	2 4/5
Guidance Counselors:	3 2/5	2 2/5
Homemaking Teachers:	2 3/5	2
Industrial Arts Teachers:	3	2 4/5
Library Librarian—A.V.A.:	1	1 1/2
Mathematics Teachers:	6 2/5	5 9/10
Music Teachers:	2	2
Physical Education Teachers:	6	5
Science Teachers:	6 3/5	6 2/5
Social Studies Teachers:	9 4/5	8 2/5
TOTALS:	58 4/5	51 9/10

It was recommended that the following be assigned to the Lakeview School in addition to the above:

1. An assistant principal each for the junior and senior high school divisions.

2. An assistant principal responsible for staff supervision and curriculum planning.

3. An assistant-to-the-principal, responsible for general administrative supervision and concerned with pupil personnel problems.

4. A dean of students, responsible for the co-curricular program and student behavior.

5. Seven secretaries to handle the non-teaching administrative operations, one each for the principal, the assistant principal, the guidance staff, the library, the attendance office and the assistant-to-the-principal, and the general office receptionist and the dean of students.

This schedule calls for classes of varying time lengths in all areas and for the large-small group sectioning in the following areas as:

Art Department
None, but extended blocks of time in all courses.

Business Education Department
Basic Business; Bookkeeping; Varying Class Lengths in all other courses.

English Department
7th Grade English; 8th Grade English; English 1, 2; English 3, 4; English 5, 6; English 7, 8; Business Communications

Foreign Language Department
Latin 1, 2; Latin 3, 4; Spanish 1, 2; Spanish 3, 4; French 1, 2; French 3, 4

Guidance Department
7th Grade; 8th Grade; 9th Grade

Homemaking Department
7th Grade; 8th Grade; Homemaking 1, 2; Clothing; Foods

Industrial Arts Department
7th Grade; 8th Grade; Industrial Arts 1, 2; Electricity; Woodworking; Drafting

Mathematics Department
General Math 1, 2; Algebra 1, 2; Plane Geometry; Solid Geometry; Trigonometry

Physical Education Department

8th Grade Boys P.E.; 7th, 8th, 9th, 10th and 11th Boys and Girls (Combined) Health with 10th only on a small group breakdown.

Science Department

8th Grade Science; Biology 1, 2; Physical Science 1, 2; Chemistry; Physics

Social Studies Department

8th Grade Social Studies; Economic Geography; World History; U.S. History; Social and Government Problems

Appendix II

Student Opinionnaire Summary

A questionnaire was given to all students in grades 9-12 concerning the Decatur-Lakeview Plan. The results were used in staff studies and in shaping administrative decisions.

QUESTION 1—*How many large group classes did you have?*

Grade 9—(mean) 9 sessions each week

Grade 10—(mean) 11 sessions each week

Grade 11—(mean) 8 sessions each week

Grade 12—(mean) 10 sessions each week

QUESTION 2—*How many subjects did you take this year?*

Grade 9—(mean) 6   Grade 11—(mean) 5

Grade 10—(mean) 5   Grade 12—(mean) 5

(This contrasted with students in the other Decatur Schools vividly. The vast majority in the other schools took only four subjects each year.)

QUESTION 3—*Please check the following scale to show in what way the large group instruction was of help to you. (5 is high and 1 shows little help.)*

Level   Mean

Grade 9—4.4

Grade 10—4.8

Grade 11—3.1

Grade 12—4.0

QUESTION 4—*Did you have the opportunity to discuss in small groups the materials covered in large groups? (Always; Usually; Rarely)*

Grade 9—Always   14% ; Usually   70% ; Rarely   16%
Grade 10—Always   3% ; Usually   60% ; Rarely   37%
Grade 11—Always   1% ; Usually   4% ; Rarely   95%
Grade 12—Always   24% ; Usually   51% ; Rarely   25%

QUESTION 5—*Was it necessary for you to assume more responsibility in small groups this year than in regular groups last year? (More; Same; Less)*

Grade 9—More   64% ; Same   23% ; Less   13%
Grade 10—More   87% ; Same   10% ; Less   3%
Grade 11—More   4% ; Same   32% ; Less   64%
Grade 12—More   14% ; Same   43% ; Less   43%

QUESTION 6—*Would you have liked to do more independent study?*

Grade 9—Yes   72% ; No   28%
Grade 10—Yes   67% ; No   33%
Grade 11—Yes   5% ; No   95%
Grade 12—Yes   81% ; No   19%

QUESTION 7—*Did you think that most students were self-directive enough to do independent study?*

Grade 9—Yes   71% ; No   29%
Grade 10—Yes   89% ; No   11%
Grade 11—Yes   79% ; No   21%
Grade 12—Yes   62% ; No   38%

QUESTION 8—*Did you feel the time spent in study here was:*

Grade 9—Too Much   19% ; Right   78% ; Not Enough   3%
Grade 10—Too Much   4% ; Right   87% ; Not Enough   9%
Grade 11—Too Much   65% ; Right   23% ; Not Enough   12%
Grade 12—Too Much   4% ; Right   80% ; Not Enough   16%

QUESTION 9—*Compared to a traditional school program, did you like the Decatur-Lakeview Plan?*

Grade 9—Better   82% ; Same   12% ; Less   6%
Grade 10—Better   79% ; Same   12% ; Less   9%
Grade 11—Better   21% ; Same   20% ; Less   59%
Grade 12—Better   86% ; Same   11% ; Less   3%

QUESTION 10—*Do you think the Decatur-Lakeview Plan will help you educationally?*

Grade 9—More   78% ; Same   18% ; Less   4%
Grade 10—More   85% ; Same   11% ; Less   4%
Grade 11—More   16% ; Same   40% ; Less   44%
Grade 12—More   66% ; Same   12% ; Less   22%

Appendix III

Questions and Answers Concerning the Decatur-Lakeview Plan

(The questions were formulated by the Lay Advisory Committee and answered by the department heads. They were distributed in the community.)

1. *What was the Decatur-Lakeview Plan?*

   . . . . It was a planned attempt to improve instruction by using:

   a. varying class sizes, small and large groups

   b. providing students with time for independent study

   c. specializing the functions of the members of a "teaching-team"

   d. re-evaluating the school's curriculum

2. *What was the purpose of the Decatur-Lakeview Plan?*

. . . . Primarily its purpose was to IMPROVE INSTRUC-
TION through emphasis on structuring an educational program for each student. It was intended to make better use of
human and financial resources and, thus, to make it possible
for the professional staff to give more expert service.

3. *How did the Plan go into operation?*

. . . . After extensive and detailed study by the staff, the
Plan was inaugurated gradually over a two-year period until
all content areas and each grade level were included.

4. *Why did Lakeview institute this program?*

. . . . Lakeview had the background of a two-year study
of the organization as suggested, the building lent itself to
change, the staff was an alert, skilled group with the ability
to accomplish the Plan's goals and the student population was
of appropriate size to put the Plan into operation on an experimental basis.

5. *How did this program benefit the teacher?*

. . . . When the teacher became a specialist in restricted
phases of instruction, he tended to be more effective. As
professional people become more effective, their services become personally more worthwhile and satisfying.

6. *Why was the Plan announced to the community a year before its inception?*

. . . . This allowed time for careful study and discussion of
the Plan by teachers with students and parents. Also, it gave
the staff time to phase into the new instructional procedures.

7. *What were the requirements and standards for the various
members of the "teaching team"?*

. . . . These were not rigidly set. The staff was expected to
be competent in its subject-matter area and interested in the
education of young adults.

8. *How were assignments of certified people on the "teaching team" made?*

. . . . These were made like all assignments in other schools, by teacher request with the principal's approval after the consultation and consent of the assistant superintendent.

9. *Did this Plan have all the features of Dr. Lloyd Trump's "Images of the Future"?*

. . . . No, it did not. There were some differences and many similarities. The Plan was a program geared to the needs of Decatur students, with Decatur teachers in mind and with adaptations of the organization for instruction felt to be in line with Lakeview students' previous learning experiences.

10. *What did this Plan provide for the Accelerated Program and the Individual Help Class Program?*

. . . . It was intended to strengthen the features of the Individual difference provisions of these programs, for the academically talented and disadvantaged learner, through the small group instruction aspect of the Plan.

11. *By whom was this Plan approved?*

. . . . By the Superintendent of Schools, by the Board of Education, by the State Department of Public Instruction and with the knowledge of the state representative of the North Central Association of Colleges and Secondary Schools.

12. *What part did small group instruction play in the Plan?*

. . . . This feature was probably the Plan's greatest strength. While much attention was attracted to large group instruction, the small group instruction may have served as the greatest benefit to students as the teacher could devote more time in these groups to the individual and his educational needs.

13. *How did this Plan influence the typical [teacher] status?*

. . . . It improved the teacher's status because he became a specialist and because the clerical chores of instruction were minimized.

14. *Did this Plan increase student control problems?*

. . . . It did not.

15. *How did students benefit from the Plan?*

. . . . From better instruction, from an emphasis on creative and independent activity, and through fuller involvement in the learning processes.

16. *Year-round school is frequently mentioned. Was this pictured in this Plan?*

. . . . No, it was not at the time. However, year-round school could or could not be carried on with this Plan for the same reasons it could or could not be carried out with the traditional organization and system of instruction.

17. *How did the faculty go about developing the Decatur-Lakeview Plan?*

. . . . In faculty, in department and cabinet meetings and during a summer workshop a united staff effort was put into developing an even better program of instruction.

18. *What has been the reaction to the Plan thus far?*

. . . . Excellent. Those with whom we have talked on the theoretical level, on the policy level and on the community level see many merits of the Plan. Its success or failure will depend on the kind of instruction given. However, people who do not understand it, can be expected to tend to resist it.

19. *Did this Plan cost the taxpayers more money than they could have been expected to spend in a traditional organization?*

. . . . No, it did not. Instead, it represented a redeployment of funds in a more efficient manner.

20. *Who was responsible for the development of this Plan?*

. . . . The Lakeview staff. The central office administrators have been interested but casual observers.

21. *Did this Plan produce mental or social "giants"?*

. . . . No, it did not. It did as good a job as we have seen done and there is the distinct possibility it has done an even better job of the development of student talents.

Appendix IV

Uses of Multimedia Teaching Aids by Departments

Department	Media	Course	Use
Art	Overhead Projector	Drawing & Painting	Step-by-step sketching demonstrations
	Magnetic Tapes	7th & 8th Grade Art	Teacher can aid students with directions given on tape
	Opaque Projector	All courses	Presentation of great works of art to accompany discussions
Business Education	Overhead Projector	Basic Business	Elementary economic principles by graphs
		Transcription	Used in place of chalk board
	Language Laboratory	Shorthand	Skill development
		Transcription	Skill development

Department	Media	Course	Use
Business Education (cont.)	Magnetic Tapes	Shorthand	Content presentation
		Basic Business	Business leader interviews
		Salesmanship	Case studies
		Business Law	Case studies
	Films	Salesmanship	Content presentation
	Film Strips	Bookkeeping	Content presentation
		Office Practice	Content presentation
	Mock-ups	Office Occupations	Motivation
		Salesmanship	Demonstration
	Skinner-type Boxes	Transcription	Fact acquisition
		Shorthand	Fact acquisition
		Business Law	Fact acquisition
	Multiple Choice	Salesmanship	Pupil evaluation
	Opaque Projector	Bookkeeping	Content presentation
		Office Practice	Machine explanation
		Basic Business	Content presentation
	Flannel Board	Typing I	Content presentation
		Business Law	Content presentation
		Salesmanship	Content presentation
		Basic Business	Content presentation
	Reading Machines	Shorthand	Skill development
		Transcription	Skill development
Driver Education	Overhead Projector	Driver Education	Content presentation
		Driver Training	Content presentation
	Magnetic Tapes	Driver Education	Lectures from police chief, etc.
	Film Strips	Driver Education	Individual examination
	Flannel Board	Driver Education	Content presentation
English	Overhead Projector	English, 7-12	Grammar presentation
	Tape Recorder	English, 7-12	Voice improvement
	Recordings	English, 7-12	Literature appreciation
	Magnetic Tapes	English, 7-12	Interviews and exchanges
	Films	English, 10-12	Literature appreciation
	Film Strips	English, 7-12	Motivation and explanation
	Multiple Choice Machines	English, 7-12	Fact reinforcement
	Skinner Boxes	English, 7-12	Fact reinforcement
	Opaque Projector	English, 7-12	Content presentation
	Reading Machines	English, 7-12	Speed and comprehension
	Flannel Boards	English, 7-12	Content demonstration
	Mitten Letters	English, 9-12	Message display
	Cut Letters	English, 7-12	Message display

Department	Media	Course	Use
Foreign Language	Language Laboratory	Spanish	Skill development
		French	Skill development
		Latin	Skill development
		Russian	Skill development
	Films	Spanish	Background information
		Latin	Background information
		French	Background information
	Film Strips	Spanish	Background information
		Latin	Background information
		French	Background information
	Magnetic Tapes	Spanish	Exchanged with students in Spain
		French	Exchanged with students in France
	Record Player, Records	French	Skill development
		Spanish	Skill development
		Latin	Skill development
	Flannel Boards	Spanish	Grammar presentation
		Latin	Grammar presentation
		French	Grammar presentation
	Opaque Projector	Spanish	Skill development
		French	Skill development
		Latin	Skill development
Home-making	Magnetic Tapes	7th & 8th Grades	Interviews from famous homemakers
	Mock-ups	Homemaking 1, 2	Motivation
	Opaque Projector	Clothing	Fashion demonstration
	Flannel Board	Family Living	Content presentation
		Home Furnishing	Home arrangement
	Opaque Projector	First Aid	Content presentation
Industrial Arts	Overhead Projector	Auto Mechanics	Demonstrations
		Industrial Arts 1, 2	Content presentation
	Magnetic Tapes	Auto Mechanics	Guest of consultant lectures
	Mock-up	Electricity	Content presentation
		Arch. Drawing	Content presentation
	Films	Industrial Arts, 1, 2	Content presentation
		Auto Mechanics	Content presentation
		Electricity	Content presentation
		Metals	Content presentation
	Film Strips	7th & 8th Grades	Content presentation
	Flannel Board	Electricity	Content demonstrations
		Auto Mechanics	Content demonstrations
		Drafting	Content demonstrations
		Industrial Arts, 1, 2	Content demonstrations

Department	Media	Course	Use
Library	Film Strips	Grades 7-8	Explanation of Dewey Decimal system
	Mock-ups	Grades 7-12	Organization of ideas
Mathematics	Overhead Projector	Algebra	Content explanation
		Plane Geometry	Content explanation
		Solid Geometry	Content explanation
		Trigonometry	Content explanation
		College Algebra	Content explanation
		Advanced Mathematics	Content explanation
	Magnetic Tapes	Grades 7-8	Skill reinforcement
	Closed Circuit TV	General Math	Large group instruction
		Grades 7-8	Large group instruction
	Films	Algebra	Motivation & explanation
	Skinner Boxes	Grades 7-8	Fact acquisition
	Multiple Choice	Grades 7-8	Skill development
	Flannel Board	Algebra	Content presentation
		Economic Mathematics	Content presentation
Music	Overhead Projector	Band	Formation direction
	Magnetic Tapes	General Music 7, 8	Music appreciation
	Recordings	General Music 7, 8	Content presentation
	Magnetic Tapes	Band	Skill development
	Flannel Board	Orchestra & Band	Content presentation
Health & Physical Education	Overhead Projector	Health, 7-12	Content presentation
	Magnetic Tapes	P.E., 9-10	Motivational interviews
	Films	Athletics (Football)	General instruction
	Flannel Board	P.E., 11-12	Game explanation
Science	Overhead Projector	Biology	Content explanation
		Grades 7-8, Gen. Science	Content explanation
	Magnetic Tapes	Grades 7-8, Gen. Science	Skill development
	Skinner Boxes	Physical Science	Fact acquisition
		Physics	Fact acquisition
	Opaque Projector	Chemistry	Content presentation
	Flannel Board	Chemistry	Content presentation
		Physics	Content presentation
	Mock-ups	Chemistry	Content presentation
	Films	Biology	Content presentation
		Grades 7-8	Content presentation
	Film Strips	Physical Science	Content presentation
		Grades 7-8, Gen. Science	Content presentation

Department	Media	Course	Use
Social Studies	Overhead Projector	Grades 7-8, Soc. St.	Content presentation
		Government Problems	Content presentation
	Films	Grade 8, Soc. St.	Content presentation
		U.S. History	Content presentation
		Social Problems	Content presentation
	Video Tapes	U.S. History	Content presentation
	Film Strips	Grade 7, Soc. St.	Content presentation
		World History	Content presentation
		U.S. History	Content presentation
	Recordings	Government Problems	Content presentation
		Social Problems	Content presentation
	Skinner Boxes	World History	Fact acquisition
		U.S. History	Fact acquisition
	Multiple Choice	Economic Geography	Fact acquisition
	Opaque Projector	Economic Geography	Content presentation
	Flannel Boards	Economic Geography	Content presentation
		U.S. History	Content presentation
		World History	Content presentation

The above are merely examples of usage and should not be construed as the limiting uses of multimedia aids.

In each case, the department chairman suggested the media and its use.

An in-service workshop was structured to give staff the knowledge and skills to use these materials.

Selected Bibliography

Books and Monographs

American Educational Research Association, "Curriculum Planning and Development," David R. Krathwohl, ed., *Review of Educational Research,* Volume 30, Number 3 (Washington, D.C., 1960), pp. 184-274.

American Educational Research Association, "Educational Organization, Administration and Finance," David R. Krathwohl, ed., *Review of Educational Research,* Volume 31, Number 4 (Washington, D.C., 1961), pp. 351-438.

Anderson, Robert, "Organizing Groups for Instruction," Nelson B. Henry ed.; *Individualizing Instruction,* The Sixty-First Yearbook of the National Society for the Study of Education (Chicago, 1962), pp. 239-264.

Beggs, David W. et al., *Team Teaching—Bold New Venture,* Unified College Press (Indianapolis, Indiana, 1964), pp. 1-208.

Bush, Robert N. and Dwight W. Allen, *A New Design for High School Education: Assuming a Flexible Schedule,* Secondary Education Project, Stanford University (Stanford, 1961), pp. 1-122.

Elam, Stanley (ed.), *Research Studies in Education,* 1960, Phi Delta Kappa (Bloomington, Illinois, 1960), pp. 1-86.

Estes, W. K., "Learning," C. W. Harris and M. R. Liba, eds., *Encyclopedia of Educational Research,* Macmillan and Company (New York, 1960), pp. 752-767.

Goodlad, John D., "The Increasing Concern for Effective Teacher Utilization," F. S. Chase and H. A. Anderson, eds., *The High School in a New Era,* University of Chicago Press (Chicago, 1958), pp. 1-350.

Heller, Melvin P. and Elizabeth Belford, *Team Teaching and Staff Utilization in Ridgewood High School,* Ridgewood Board of Education (Norridge, Illinois, 1960), pp. 1-18.

Hilgard, Ernest R., "Learning Theory and Its Application," *New Teaching Aids for the American Classroom,* Institute for Communications Research (Stanford, 1960), pp. 19-27.

Kingsley, Howard L. and Ralph Garry, *The Nature and Conditions of Learning,* Prentice-Hall, Inc. (Englewood Cliffs, N.J., 1957), pp. 1-521.

Lear, John, "A New Look at the Human Mind," *Saturday Review* (April, 1961), pp. 39-41.

Lobb, Delbert, *An Experimental Study of Means of Improving the Utilization of the Staff in the Secondary Schools,* Report of Jefferson County, Colorado, School System (Colorado, 1959), pp. 1-35.

Lobb, Delbert, *A Report of a Three Year Study,* Jefferson County, Colorado, School System (Colorado, 1960), pp. 1-30.

Morse, Arthur D., "Team Teaching in Action: The Franklin School in Lexington, Massachusetts," *Schools of Tomorrow—Today,* Doubleday and Co. (New York, 1960), pp. 9-26.

Research Division of the National Education Association, "Abstracts of Reported Studies of Reorganization of the Professional Staff," in *Studies of Utilization of Staff, Buildings, and Audio Visual Aids in the Public Schools,* National Education Association (Washington, D.C., 1959), pp. 1-24.

Trump, J. Lloyd, *Images of the Future: A New Approach to the Secondary Schools,* National Association of Secondary School Principals (Washington D.C., 1959), pp. 1-46.

Trump, J. Lloyd, *New Directions to Quality Education,* National Association of Secondary School Principals (Washington, D.C., 1960), pp. 1-14.

Trump, J. Lloyd and Dorsey Baynham, *Focus on Change,* Rand-McNally (Chicago, 1961), pp. 1-147.

United States Office of Education, *Cooperative Research Projects, Bulletin*

1961, Number 18, United States Government Printing Office (Washington, D.C., 1961), pp. 1-40.

Vinacke, W. Edgar, *The Psychology of Thinking,* McGraw-Hill (New York, 1957), pp. 1-361.

Wall, Harvey R. and Robert W. Reasoner, *Team Teaching: A Descriptive and Evaluative Study of a Program for the Primary Grades,* Mt. Diablo School District (Concord, California, 1962), pp. 1-131.

Wrightstone, J. Wayne, "Class Organization for Instruction," *What Research Says to the Teacher,* Department of Classroom Teachers and the American Educational Research Association of the National Education Association (Washington, D.C., 1957), pp. 1-142.

Periodicals

National Association of Secondary-School Principals Bulletin, "New Horizons in Staff Utilization," Volume 42 (January, 1958), pp. 1-213.

National Association of Secondary-School Principals Bulletin, "Exploring Improved Teaching Patterns," Volume 43 (January, 1959), pp. 1-348.

National Association of Secondary-School Principals Bulletin, "Progressing Toward Better Schools," Volume 44 (January, 1960), pp. 1-380.

National Association of Secondary-School Principals Bulletin, "Seeking Improved Learning Opportunities," Volume 45 (January, 1961), pp. 1-352.

National Association of Secondary-School Principals Bulletin, "Locus of Change," Volume 46 (January, 1962), pp. 1-360.

National Association of Secondary-School Principals Bulletin, Volume 47 (May, 1963).

Anderson, Robert H., "Team Teaching in Action," *Nation's Schools,* Volume 65 (May, 1960), pp. 62-65.

Anrig, Gregory R., "Promising and Perplexing Aspects of Large Group Teaching Experiments," *The Bulletin of the National Association of Secondary School Principals,* Volume 46 (January, 1962), pp. 253-260.

Beggs, David W., "A Success Story of Small and Large Group Instruction: The Decatur-Lakeview Plan," *Overview,* Volume 3, No. 12 (December, 1962), pp. 42-48.

Bush, Robert N., "Team Teaching Bandwagon" (editorial), *California Journal of Secondary Education,* Volume 35 (April, 1960), pp. 207-208.

Cunningham, Lavern, "Team Teaching: Where Do We Stand?" *Administrators Notebook,* Volume 8 (March, 1960), pp. 1-4.

Drummond, H. D., "Team Teaching: An Assessment," *Educational Leadership,* Volume 19 (December, 1961), pp. 160-165.

Gale, R. F., "Comparative Study of College Experiences of Graduates of the Core and of the Conventional Curricula," *Journal of Experimental Education,* Volume 27 (January, 1959), pp. 283-296.

Goodlad, John L., "Experiment in Team Teaching," *Elementary School Journal,* Volume 59 (October, 1958), pp. 11-13.

Hough, John B., "Research Vindication for Teaching Machines," *Phi Delta Kappan,* Volume XLIII (March, 1962), pp. 240-243.

Lear, John, "A New Look at the Human Mind," *Saturday Review* (April, 1961), pp. 39-41.

Ohm, Robert E., "Toward a Rationale for Team Teaching," *Administrators Notebook,* Volume 9 (March, 1961), pp. 1-4.

Olds, Henry F., "Survey of a Meeting on Team Teaching," *Minutes,* (Committee on Team Teaching), Chicago (March, 1961), pp. 1-8.

Pitruzzello, Philip R., "A Report on Team Teaching," *Clearing House,* Volume 36 (February, 1962), pp. 333-336.

Ploghft, M. E. "Another Look at Team Teaching," *Clearing House,* Volume 36 (December, 1961), pp. 219-221.

Siegel, L., and others, "Effectiveness of Large Group Instruction at the University Level," *Harvard Educational Review,* Volume 29 (Summer, 1959), pp. 216-226.

Symposium: "Using Team Teaching to Individualize Instruction," *Journal of Secondary Education,* Volume 36 (November, 1961), pp. 414-446.

Szabo, L. J., "Team Teaching: Honors Students Undergo Experiments," *New York State Education,* Volume 49 (September, 1961), pp. 12-13.

Taylor, Harris A., "Claremont Graduate School Program for Team Teaching," *High School Journal,* Volume 43 (February, 1960), pp. 277-282.

Trump, J. Lloyd, "Quality Education of the Future," *Frontiers of Education,* Report of the Twenty-seventh Educational Conference, Educational Records Bureau (November, 1962), pp. 23-39.

Index